SECRET APPALACHIAN HIGHLANDS

A Guide to the Weird, Wonderful, and Obscure

Robert Sorrell

Reedy Press
PO Box 5131
St. Louis, MO 63139
reedypress.com

Library of Congress Control Number: 2024930400
ISBN: 9781681065267

Design by Jill Halpin

Unless otherwise indicated, all photos are courtesy of the author or in the public domain.

We (the publisher and the author) have done our best to provide the most accurate information available when this book was completed. However, we make no warranty, guarantee, or promise about the accuracy, completeness, or currency of the information provided, and we expressly disclaim all warranties, express or implied. Please note that attractions, company names, addresses, websites, and phone numbers are subject to change or closure, and this is outside of our control. We are not responsible for any loss, damage, injury, or inconvenience that may occur due to the use of this book. When exploring new destinations, please do your homework before you go. You are responsible for your own safety and health when using this book.

Printed in the United States of America
24 25 26 27 28   5 4 3 2 1

For my wife, Dalena

Lost Cove

CONTENTS

Wild pony

ACKNOWLEDGMENTS

I would like to thank my friends and family for their support during this project, and for all their suggestions, ideas, and stories offered for inclusion in the book. Many people told me of things that I was not aware of, nor ever heard of.

Much of this book is based on local history and I would like to thank the local historians, historical societies, and archivists who helped with the project and provided documentation and photographs. Contributing historical organizations include the Heritage Alliance; the Rogersville Heritage Association; Watauga Historical Association; Bristol Historical Association; Kingsport Archives; Unicoi County Historical Society; Washington County Tennessee Archives; the Boone's Creek Museum and Opry; Traditional Voices Group; and the Historical Society of Washington County, Virginia.

I also want to thank the local chambers of commerce and tourism organizations that provided a great deal of information and many photographs. Contributing tourism-related organizations include Visit Johnson City, Scott County Tourism, Explore Bristol, the Heart of Appalachia Tourism Authority, and the Town of Big Stone Gap.

Several venues, attractions, and businesses—many mentioned throughout the book—have been very helpful. Other contributors include USA Raft Adventures, the Carter Family Fold, the Barter Theatre, the Paramount Center for the Arts, General Shale Brick, the Elizabethton-Carter County Public Library, the Butler Museum, Backyard Terrors, the Birthplace of Country Music, George L. Carter Railroad Museum, and the Unicoi County Public Library.

Additional contributors have included Laken Branson, Stanford Dailey, Lisa Germaine, and Alex Garrison.

"Wagon Wheel" mural
in Johnson City

INTRODUCTION

One might expect a historic region tucked into the hills and valleys of the Appalachian Mountains to have some weird, wonderful, and obscure treasures. The Appalachian Highlands, a region consisting of the communities of Northeast Tennessee and Southwest Virginia, has more than its share of strange, quirky, and unique places. In many cases, those places are also dripping with history and heritage, oftentimes dating back centuries.

The core of the Appalachian Highlands region is comprised of what locals call the Tri-Cities, which includes Bristol, a city home to the not-so-obscure Bristol Motor Speedway; Johnson City, a world-class university town; and Kingsport, the center of industry for the region.

A drive around the Tri-Cities might raise a few questions, like, why is an airplane that seems to have crashed into the side of a hill along Interstate 26 still there? Why can visitors find not just one but two giant Native American statues in the Tri-Cities? Who might have stayed in that luxury apartment building?

Leave the cities and discover the region's many quaint and picturesque small towns and the rural countryside. This guidebook takes visitors and locals to the towns of Elizabethton, Greeneville, Rogersville, and Erwin in Tennessee, as well as the Virginia towns of Abingdon, Norton, Big Stone Gap, and others.

While visiting the rural Appalachian Highlands, visitors might ask: Did they really punish criminals at the pillory? Why are there a bunch of wolves in Abingdon? What is a Woodbooger?

Several famous residents like Tennessee Ernie Ford and Eliza McCardle Johnson, as well as guests like Hank Williams Sr., are featured in this guidebook.

This book uncovers many of the region's secrets, and also includes a few ghost stories, mysteries, and legends. Oh, and there is a horse, of course.

FIRST LADY'S BIRTHPLACE

Where is former First Lady Eliza McCardle Johnson buried?

No, former First Lady Eliza McCardle Johnson is not buried in Telford, Tennessee, but it is easy to understand why one might be confused!

Johnson, the wife of Andrew Johnson, the 17th president of the United States, is buried in the national cemetery in Greeneville. The couple is buried atop Monument Hill with other family members, including Eliza's mother, Sarah Phillips-McCardle.

A monument recognizing her birth, however, can be found among the grave sites at the McCarty United Methodist Church and Cemetery in Telford. The Leesburg Ruritan Club and the Sarah Hawkins chapter of the Daughters of the American Revolution established the marker in 1976.

ELIZA JOHNSON MONUMENT

WHAT: The birthplace of President Andrew Johnson's wife

WHERE: 104 McCarty Church Rd., Telford, TN 37690

COST: Free

PRO TIP: Be sure to check out the cemetery's oldest graves.

The site is the birthplace of the former first lady. She was born on October 4, 1810, to a shoemaker father, John, and his homemaker wife, Sarah. Her family later gave land for the church and cemetery in 1821.

The family relocated to the town of Greeneville. After the death of her father, Eliza and Sarah supported themselves by making and selling quilts and leather goods.

Family tradition holds that in September 1826, a young Eliza saw young Andrew Johnson leading a blind pony hitched to a

Eliza McCardle Johnson's birth marker is located in McCarty Cemetery in rural Telford, Tennessee.

small cart into town and commented to her friends, "There goes my beau, girls, mark it."

Andrew and Eliza were married on May 17, 1827. The couple eventually owned a few houses in Greeneville. Andrew Johnson knew his letters and could read a bit, so his wife, Eliza, who was well educated, taught the future president writing and arithmetic.

Andrew's successful transition from tailor to politician began in 1829, when he was elected town alderman. He later became a town mayor, state representative, and US representative. He became president in 1865 upon the death of Abraham Lincoln.

Eliza died on January 15, 1876.

DIVERS' PARADISE

Why is there still a visible airplane crash site along the side of the interstate in Gray?

Drive along Interstate 26 in the Gray, Tennessee, area, and you might spot an airplane that appears to have crashed into the side of a cliff.

You can only spot the airplane while heading west between Johnson City and Kingsport near Exit 13.

But no worries. The airplane was placed there as part of Gray Quarry, a diver's paradise in the heart of Northeast Tennessee.

The property, previously owned by the Gray family, became a rock quarry in the 1960s as part of the construction of the local highway system. A diver later purchased the property in 2005 and planned to develop a diving quarry.

Eventually, a group of diving enthusiasts purchased the property and developed the current Gray Quarry, a spot for divers to explore the unknown.

Organizers have sunk several items into the quarry, including a boat, plane, fire truck, school, and statues. Divers will also find a variety of fish in the water.

The quarry features a nearly three-acre, 70-foot-deep lake. The water remains at a constant temperature due to continuous aeration, making it a comfortable spot for diving.

Bigfoot can be seen wandering around the edge of Gray Quarry, which can be found near Interstate 26.

GRAY QUARRY

WHAT: Gray Quarry is a popular diving spot.

WHERE: 169 Buckingham Rd., Johnson City, TN 37615

COST: $15 per day

PRO TIP: Visit grayquarry.com to make reservations and sign a liability waiver.

Those using the quarry must do so at their own risk. There's no one on duty.

Since Gray Quarry is not a staffed facility, divers must sign waivers and pay daily dive fees through partnering dive shops, which can be found across the region as well as in North Carolina. According to the organization, fee proceeds are then used to maintain and upgrade the quarry.

LADY AND THE *DOUGHBOY*

What do two seemingly unlike Johnson City statues have in common?

Drive around Johnson City and you're likely to encounter several pieces of art, including murals, memorials, and statues. There are two statues in particular—located roughly one mile away from each other—that share a relatively common theme: veterans.

In 1904, in honor of former Congressman Walter Preston Brownlow, *Lady of the Fountain* was placed in downtown Johnson City. The bronze statue, which has seen its fair share of movement over the years, is today located at the intersection of Buffalo and Main Streets in what is known as Fountain Square, according to historian Bob Cox.

Brownlow was responsible for Johnson City being selected in 1901 as the site of the Mountain Branch of the National Home for Disabled Volunteer Veterans, which is today an active Veterans Affairs hospital, with grounds also worth a visit.

HISTORIC JOHNSON CITY MONUMENTS

WHAT: Two separate downtown monuments dedicated to America's veterans

WHERE: Fountain Square at the corner of Buffalo and Main Streets; Veterans Plaza on Bert Street

COST: Free

PRO TIP: Visit downtown Johnson City in the evening for a great meal and a show at one of the nearby venues.

Spirit of the American Doughboy in Johnson City is the only genuine Ernest Moore Viquesney statue in Tennessee, according to an online database.

The Lady of the Fountain *and* Spirit of the American Doughboy *statues were first installed in the downtown Johnson City, Tennessee, area to recognize the community's veterans.*

The congressman had sympathized with the plight of older Union Civil War veterans maimed during the war and shamefully reduced to mere homeless beggars.

As a result, the city's leaders reportedly chose to honor the congressman with a statue to be placed in the heart of the city. The statue was fabricated in a New York City foundry and delivered to the city. Due to construction and wear on the statue, she has moved a couple times but remains downtown, Cox said.

Another statue, known as *Spirit of the American Doughboy*, can be found along Main Street near the Memorial Park Community Center. Crafted by Ernest Moore Viquesney, the *Doughboy* statue was installed and dedicated in Johnson City in 1935. They became popular and Viquesney built copper *Doughboy* statues for communities across the country.

The *Doughboy* was erected to honor American military personnel who died in World War I. Since then, additional inscriptions have been included to recognize the dead of World War II, Korea, Vietnam, and other wars.

MOUNTAIN DEW

Where was Mountain Dew invented?

One of the world's most popular soft drinks was formulated and bottled in the Appalachian Highlands.

An historical marker in Johnson City, Tennessee, at the corner of Walnut and Cherokee Streets notes the community's connection with Mountain Dew. The sign marks the former site of the Tri-City Beverage Corporation, a company that was owned by Charles O. Gordon.

The beverage had originally been created by Knoxville, Tennessee, brothers Barney and Ally Hartman and patented by Hartman Beverage Company in 1948. In 1954, the company became one of the first to bottle Mountain Dew, a clear lemon-lime drink, according to the Tennessee Historical Commission marker.

Four years later, Plant Manager Bill Bridgeforth developed a new citrus-lemonade-flavored drink called Tri-City Lemonade. In 1960, he placed his lemonade drink into the Mountain Dew bottles, which is the flavor in Mountain Dew today.

The right to the formula was obtained by the Tip Corporation of Marion, Virginia, which further developed the beverage.

Bill Jones, with the Tip Corporation, took the recipe and added "secret" ingredients to make it into one of the top-selling soft drinks worldwide, according to a marker in Marion. In 1964, Pepsi-Cola acquired the Mountain Dew brand.

MOUNTAIN DEW

WHAT: Marker dedicated to the history of Mountain Dew

WHERE: 800 block of W Walnut St., Johnson City, TN 37604

COST: Free

PRO TIP: Read the book *Mountain Dew: Hillbilly Collectables* by Dick Bridgforth and Wayne Burgess to learn more about the popular soda and its connection to the Appalachian Highlands.

A Tennessee Historical Commission marker recognizes Johnson City, Tennessee, as the home of Mountain Dew. Photo courtesy of Washington County Archives.

In 2012, Pepsi introduced a new Mountain Dew called Johnson City Gold.

More information and artifacts about Mountain Dew and Dr. Enuf, another local beverage, can be found at the Reece Museum at East Tennessee State University.

“WAGON WHEEL”

How do I get to Johnson City from Cumberland Gap?

“So, rock me mama like a wagon wheel / Rock me mama any way you feel . . .”

Those iconic lyrics are featured in the song “Wagon Wheel,” a country music hit, written by legends Bob Dylan and Ketch Secor of Old Crow Medicine Show. Secor’s band released the song in 2004 and it became an instant classic. Darius Rucker released his own version of “Wagon Wheel” in 2013, and it also became a hit.

Play the song in Northeast Tennessee, and there is one particular line residents will sing at the top of their lungs: “But he’s a-headin’ west from the Cumberland Gap to Johnson City, Tennessee.”

The song describes a journey through the south, taking listeners to Roanoke, Virginia; Cumberland Gap; and Johnson City, Tennessee. Raleigh, North Carolina, is the intended final destination.

To note, Johnson City is east of Cumberland Gap, not west as the song states. Secor, who cowrote the song, said, “I got some geography wrong, but I still sing it that way. I just wanted the word ‘west’ in there. ‘West’ has got more power than ‘east.’”

As a result of the song’s popularity, it has become a country music staple in Johnson City. So much so that local artist Marci Berkhimer created a mural inspired by “Wagon Wheel.” It can be found in the Downtown Square breezeway in Johnson City.

“ROCK ME, MAMA, LIKE A WAGON WHEEL.”

WHAT: The song that put Johnson City on the map

WHERE: 216 E Main St., Johnson City, TN 37604

COST: Free

PRO TIP: Be sure to also check out the Rich-R-Tone Records historic marker and the Down Home venue for more music nostalgia.

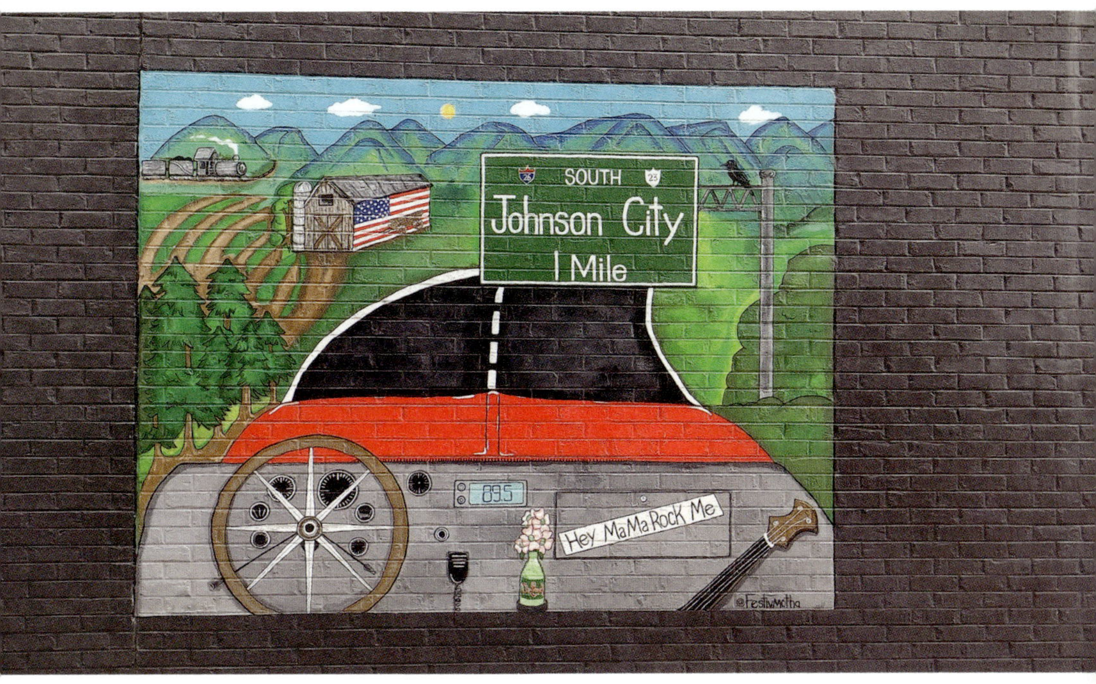

"Wagon Wheel" has become a country music staple in Johnson City, Tennessee, and is showcased in a downtown mural.

"Something about Johnson City, Tennessee, has always been captivating to us," Old Crow Medicine Show wrote on social media after learning about the mural. "All these years later that town still pulls at our heartstrings. Thanks, JC, for letting us make an official mark on the town with this mural. Even bigger thanks to FestivMotha for creating it. We're mighty proud to have just a little corner of your town to call home!"

URBAN MOUNTAIN BIKING

Looking for a place to mountain bike in the city?

The 40-acre Tannery Knobs Mountain Bike Park in Johnson City is the perfect spot to test your skills.

The heavily wooded park features off-road biking trails for all skill levels, from beginner to expert. It is located near the heart of downtown Johnson City and Interstate 26. All the trails start at the top, which overlooks the city and provides scenic views of the nearby baseball stadium and Buffalo Mountain.

First opened in the summer of 2009, Tannery Knobs has become one of the best mountain-biking destinations of the South. At the top, bicyclists can either catch one of the adrenaline-inducing trails or take on the paved pump track.

Pump tracks are innovative park amenities trending around the country. They're ideal for wheeled sports equipment such as bicycles, and when ridden properly, do not require pedaling or pushing. Instead, riders must create a "pumping" action to maintain momentum on the pump track.

A trail sign with a map can be found at the top of the park and provides a list of trail names and the designated difficulty level. The city-maintained trails include green loops for beginners all the way to the more seasoned adrenaline junkies, who can use the black loops.

The Appalachian Highlands region is home to several bicycling trails, including Tannery Knobs, the Hampton Watershed Trails in Northeast Tennessee, and Spearhead Trails in Southwest Virginia.

Head to Tannery Knobs in Johnson City, Tennessee, for a fun mountain-bike ride and a spectacular view of the nearby mountains. Photo courtesy of Visit Johnson City.

Each trail features obstacles such as well-kept rock structures, berms, jumps, and smooth surface paths. Perhaps best of all, each trail starts and finishes at the top of the park.

This is a park you'll want to visit more than once. There are several loops, allowing for new experiences every time, especially since Johnson City plans to further develop Tannery Knobs.

TANNERY KNOBS MOUNTAIN BIKE PARK

WHAT: The Tannery Knobs Mountain Bike Park features mountain-biking trails for all ages and skill levels.

WHERE: 18 Tannery Knob, Johnson City, TN 37601

COST: Free

PRO TIP: Beginners should start on the green trail. The black trails are for the more experienced bicyclists.

MINIATURE TRAINS

Where is the region's largest train display?

The region's largest miniature train display can be found at the Johnson City Railroad Experience, which continues to expand and add new exhibits.

Annually, thousands of people visit the Johnson City museum, a well-kept secret that was originally located on the campus of East Tennessee State University. The museum relocated in 2023 to an off-campus site at 207 North Boone Street that includes model trains and vintage collectibles.

The museum is staffed by volunteer docents from the Mountain Empire Model Railroaders club who staff the museum and can tell patrons all about local railroads and building your own miniature railroad village.

The museum has generated a lot of interest from railroad buffs, including members of the George L. Carter Chapter of the National Railway Historical Society and the East Tennessee & Western North Carolina Railroad Historical Society.

In 1909, according to the museum website, state officials seeking to build a teachers' college in the area, approached George L. Carter, founder of the Clinchfield Railroad, who responded generously by donating his farm and $100,000 to start what is now known as East Tennessee State University. The museum has housed three operating

JOHNSON CITY RAILROAD EXPERIENCE

WHAT: The railroad museum in Johnson City features some of the best miniature train displays in the country.

WHERE: 207 N Boone St., Johnson City, TN 37604

COST: Contact museum for current admission price.

PRO TIP: Visit johnsoncityrailroadexperience.org for the latest information on the museum.

A customized locomotive on the Mountain Empire Model Railroaders' HO-scale layout is pictured here at the museum, which relocated in 2023. Photo courtesy of Dr. Fred Alsop.

model train layouts, including one depicting Southern Appalachia in the summer; one showcasing Knoxville, Tennessee; and another depicting a 19th-century Western sawmill town.

The club has also been working on a replica of the East Tennessee & Western North Carolina Railroad. Better known as the Tweetsie Railroad, the line once stretched through the mountains from Johnson City to the mines at Cranberry, North Carolina. Primarily a narrow-gauge line, the beloved railroad passed through some of the most beautiful scenery in the area.

Upon completion, the Tweetsie model set will be the largest layout of the railroad in the world.

The museum is open five days a week at its downtown location.

The railroad museum features exhibits devoted to George L. Carter, the organization's namesake, and his Clinchfield Railroad.

OLD BRICKS

Want to take a selfie with some ancient bricks?

Surprisingly, the ancient bricks on display at the headquarters of General Shale, one of North America's top brick manufacturers, provides a popular background for selfies.

The General Shale Museum of Ancient Brick showcases 85 bricks from around the world, some dating back as far as 10,000 years ago. This one-of-a-kind museum features bricks from ancient China and Jericho, as well as Washington, DC, and Plymouth, Massachusetts.

This unique collection was curated by late General Shale employee Basil Saffer, who died in 2011. He spent decades on excursions around the world in search of rare and unique bricks.

"To me, these are not just bricks—they are pieces of history," Saffer said, according to a museum brochure. "Here you can see bricks that have been exposed for centuries and yet show no sign of wear. These things have withstood the test of time."

The museum features numerous ancient bricks, including one from the Colosseum in Rome, Italy, and another from the Great Wall of China. The museum also features a brick from the Church of St. John in Ephesus, Turkey, said to be the birthplace of Mary, the mother of Jesus. The church was built in the sixth century.

The General Shale Museum of Ancient Brick attracts history buffs from all interest groups, showcasing such finds as a brick from the Great Wall of China in the same room with one from the building where Babe Ruth was born. The museum is located in the company's lobby and open to the public.

GENERAL SHALE MUSEUM OF ANCIENT BRICK

WHAT: The ancient brick museum features some of the rarest bricks in the world.

WHERE: 3015 Bristol Hwy., Johnson City, TN 37601

COST: Free, but donations accepted

PRO TIP: The museum is in the lobby of the General Shale corporate headquarters.

An array of old bricks can be found at the gallery inside General Shale Brick in Johnson City, Tennessee. Photos courtesy of General Shale Brick.

A first-century brick from Bath, England; a brick produced in 1793 while the White House was being built; and one of the original bricks from the Appomattox, Virginia, town hall are also featured at the museum along with a brick that was shipped across the ocean on the Mayflower in 1620 and another from the biblical city of Jericho that is possibly 9,000 to 10,000 years old, according to the brochure.

TESLA COIL

Why is there a Tesla coil at the Hands On! Discovery Center?

Visitors to the science museum can witness an electrifying, musical, and Guinness World Record–breaking experience. The coil, donated to the museum in 2014, honors Nikola Tesla, who is credited with more than 250 inventions.

The coil at the Hands On! site turns 240 volts of electricity into 200,000 volts of musical lightning. It uses lightning bolts to play 18 different songs, according to the museum literature.

Tesla, who lived from 1856 to 1942, is most remembered for his technical advances with alternating current. His inventions paved the way for many modern electronics, such as radios, remote controls, fluorescent lights, cell phones, and hydro-powered dams.

The Tesla Experience, which showcases the coil, is repeated throughout the day for $2 per person with admission.

THE RECORD-BREAKING TESLA COIL

WHAT: Experience the record-breaking Tesla coil at Hands On!

WHERE: 1212 Suncrest Dr., Gray, TN 37615

COST: $11 adult general admission plus $2 for the Tesla experience. Children 3 and under are admitted for free.

PRO TIP: The Gray Fossil Site is included with Hands On! Discovery Center admission.

The coil in the Tesla Experience at the Hands On! Discovery Center can perform 18 songs, including "Under the Sea" from Disney's 1989 film, *The Little Mermaid*, and "Rocky Top," a song made popular by the Osborne Brothers.

The record-breaking Tesla coil, seen here, uses lightning bolts to play 18 different songs. Photo courtesy of Visit Johnson City.

In 2014, the coil was named the Most Powerful Musical Bi-Polar Coil by *Guinness World Records*.

Along with the Tesla coil, the museum features a variety of fun interactive programs and experiences, such as the giant building blocks, the Gray Fossil Site, and a three-story Paleo Tower.

The Gray Fossil Site, which is operated by East Tennessee State University, was established after construction crews discovered an amazing cache of fossils on the site in 2000. The active fossil dig dates back five million years. Experts have found tapirs, a red panda, a rhinoceros, a 10-ton mastodon, and many more fossils. The fossil site and museum opened in 2007, and Hands On! relocated to the Gray site in 2018.

GANGSTER'S PARADISE

Did mobsters rule Johnson City in the 1920s?

There's no evidence to support this story, but local lore says that mobsters, including the infamous Al Capone, visited and worked in Johnson City in the 1920s. Capone is said to have stayed at Montrose Court, a luxury apartment complex built in the Southwest Addition in 1922.

Designed by D.R. Beeson Jr., the 28-apartment Montrose Court was built at a cost of about $200,000. That figure was impressive at the time, primarily due to the high-quality construction techniques and materials. The Tudor-style building was hailed as the ultimate in luxury living, according to a newspaper article published in May 1922.

Capone and his men are said to have traveled to Johnson City from Chicago and Miami via the railroad. The city served as a stopover point along the route and a place for gangsters, like Capone, to hide from the law.

The city's reputation for illegal activities also gave Johnson City the nickname "Little Chicago." The bootlegging, gambling, and general disobedience associated with Prohibition were generally accepted here, according to newspaper articles in the 1920s.

The John Sevier Hotel, which opened in 1924 and currently serves as a low-income housing facility, also has been associated with organized crime figures, including Capone. In addition, the former Windsor Hotel, in operation in downtown Johnson City

---

Montrose Court, John Sevier Hotel, and Windsor Hotel in Johnson City were known for various vice activities. All but the Windsor Hotel remain standing.

from 1909 to 1971, had a reputation as a melting pot of vice activities, according to the Johnson's Depot website.

Johnson City has also been known for its underground passageways and speakeasy establishments. However, research suggests that those passageways or "escape routes" were more likely to be just water pumps and storage areas.

Be sure to visit the Windsor Speakeasy, a modern-day hideaway bar in downtown. Enjoy a cocktail in this 1930s-era attraction.

Montrose Court, located in the historic Tree Streets neighborhood between downtown Johnson City and East Tennessee State University, remains occupied by tenants.

LITTLE CHICAGO

WHAT: Gangster Al Capone may have lived at historic Montrose Court.

WHERE: 1100 block of Boyd St., Johnson City, TN 37604

COST: Free

PRO TIP: Be sure to visit the Windsor Speakeasy in downtown Johnson City. Learn more on the secret establishment's social media pages.

Historic Montrose Court apartments in Johnson City, Tennessee, may have been briefly home to Al Capone, the infamous Chicago mobster.

DANIEL BOONE "CILLED A BAR"

How do we know that Daniel Boone killed a bear in Northeast Tennessee in the 1700s?

Early American pioneer Daniel Boone blazed trails across the country. On one of his expeditions through Northeast Tennessee, he killed a bear. He carved the inscription: "D. Boon cilled a bar" (as written) on a tree in the year 1760.

The beech tree, which was located in the present-day Boones Creek community, was a big tourist attraction in the late 1800s and early 1900s. People came from afar to see where Boone killed the bear.

A storm finally took down the tree in 1916 and it was harvested. The Daughters of the American Revolution eventually acquired the wood, which was taken to local factories to be crafted into souvenir items. Some of those items were made at the old Wolfe Brothers Furniture Factory in Piney Flats—at least one Boone gavel is owned by a Wolfe descendent.

In all, about 500 gavels were produced and given to dignitaries around the country, including presidents.

One of those gavels is now on display at the Washington County Archives on Main Street in Jonesborough. It can be viewed in the lobby during normal business hours.

A state historic marker on Tennessee State Route 36 pays homage to Boone's adventures in the region. It states: "0.2 miles

---

Where was the Daniel Boone tree? It was located in the woods off present-day Old Gray Station Road, according to Washington County's deputy archivist.

Frontiersman Daniel Boone is said to have carved his initials into a tree near Johnson City, Tennessee, after killing a bear. The tree, pictured to the left, was later used to create various souvenirs. Photo courtesy of the National Archives.

along this road is the waterfall under which Boone hid himself from raiding Indians; the falls were then about 4 feet high. 1.1 mile along the road, a marker indicates the site of the beech tree where 'D. Boon cilled a bar in year 1760.'"

The Boones Creek Historical Trust maintains a large collection of historical artifacts from the Boones Creek community and Boone's adventures. The organization operates a museum and "opry" house on Hales Chapel Road.

There are also several historic monuments in the region that mark Boone's expeditions. Markers can be found in Kingsport, Bristol, Jonesborough, Johnson City, Abingdon, and Elizabethton.

DANIEL BOONE VISITS NORTHEAST TENNESSEE

WHAT: Pioneer Daniel Boone carved an inscription into a tree in Boones Creek in 1760.

WHERE: The tree is no longer standing, but you can learn more at the Boones Creek Historical Trust at 632 Hales Chapel Rd., Johnson City, TN, 37615.

COST: Free

PRO TIP: Visit the Washington County Archives in Jonesborough to see a piece of history related to Daniel Boone's tree carving plus other local historical artifacts.

THE OPRY

Looking for a fun Saturday night of Appalachian music?

Have you been to the Opry? No, not the one in Nashville, but the one in Boones Creek, Tennessee. Each Saturday, dozens of people head to the barn at the historic Keebler-Keefauver farm for an old-fashioned musical performance.

The Boones Creek Historical Trust, which operates a museum and the Opry, is a not-for-profit organization dedicated to preserving the history and culture of Boones Creek and East Tennessee. To accomplish the goal, the trust established the museum as a depository of regional material, culture, and history.

The museum is located in a beautiful brick farmhouse built in 1859. The interactive exhibits surround visitors with the echoes of Appalachian heritage, and more particularly the history of Boones Creek and its namesake, early American pioneer and trailblazer Daniel Boone.

BOONES CREEK MUSEUM AND OPRY

WHAT: The Boones Creek Opry hosts performances every Saturday night.

WHERE: 632 Hales Chapel Rd., Johnson City, TN 37615

COST: $4 and additional donations accepted.

PRO TIP: This attraction not only features a museum and music venue, but you can also learn how to play various instruments, like the dulcimer.

Musicians from around the world have performed at the Boones Creek Opry in Washington County, Tennessee. Photos courtesy of the Boones Creek Opry.

The Opry, which received a large donation from the state in 2022 to expand the facility, originally began as a community effort to celebrate, study, and preserve intangible aspects of Tennessee culture and folklife. It serves as a meeting hall, classroom, and musical training center.

Local musicians, including those from East Tennessee State University's bluegrass department, perform each Saturday night in the barn. The Opry gives musicians an opportunity to learn from each other and exchange ideas.

Following scheduled performances, the Opry serves as an open mic venue, where anyone is allowed to play the stage.

The Opry is growing. It now seats about 120 people and features one stage. The expanded site will seat about 300 people and include multiple stages.

In addition to serving as the current performance hall for the Opry, the barn also displays several permanent art installations. The floor of the future foyer features a quilt pattern depicting folklife scenes from Boones Creek, according to the historical trust. The massive painting was created by artist Vicki Shell and a team of dedicated volunteers.

An eight-foot carved mural of *Daniel Boone and the Axe Men* by Joe Pilkington can be found on the Boones Creek Opry barn's back wall.

THE PILLORY OF JONESBOROUGH

Where and how were criminals punished in Jonesborough?

Public punishment was commonplace in the 19th century in the Appalachian Highlands. People were hanged, branded, whipped, and detained, oftentimes in front of dozens if not hundreds of local residents.

In Jonesborough, the state's oldest town and seat of government for Washington County, the courthouse square served as a prime spot to host political rallies, historic anniversaries, and festivals, as well as to publicly punish criminals.

In "The Washington County Court-House, A History," Ned Irwin said public hangings were held at the rear of the courthouse. They became "major public spectacles," Irwin said. The courthouse also had a pillory, which is a wooden stand with two horizontal pieces of wood, the top of which raises and lowers. Both pieces have cut-out semicircles that, when pushed together, accommodate a person's head and hands, holding him/her immobile. Persons who were pilloried were often abused, either verbally or physically, by local bystanders.

In one case, described as a severe sentence for perjury, a man stood at the pillory for about an hour with his ears nailed to the wood. Once his time was complete, the ears were to be cut off and left nailed until sunset.

Visitors today won't see any signs of those public punishments at the courthouse, but head on over to the visitors center, and

---

In addition to the pillory, early East Tennessee furniture is on display at Jonesborough's history museum at the visitors center.

Want to see the old pillory in Jonesborough, Tennessee? It's located near the parking lot of the town's visitors center.

PUBLIC PUNISHMENT

WHAT: A wooden pillory can be found at the Jonesborough Visitors Center.

WHERE: 117 Boone St., Jonesborough, TN 37659

COST: Free

PRO TIP: Check out the Jonesborough-Washington County History Museum while stopping by the pillory in the visitors center.

there is a pillory on display. It has become an obscure yet popular spot for a photo op.

The wood pillory once stood in front of the old courthouse.

It's unknown when the original pillory was replaced, but a replica was installed during the 20th century. During courthouse renovations in the mid-1980s, another replica was built and installed at the site, according to an article in the *Johnson City Press*. The replica that had been on the site was rotting away, the article states.

Craftsman Jamie MacRae built the new punishment device and he was determined to do justice to historical accuracy. His finishing touches included distress marks to give the appearance that the device had been in place for many years, the article states.

MacRae's replica eventually was moved to the visitors center on Boone Street, a few blocks away from the historic courthouse.

DUNCAN'S ROADSIDE GRAVE

Why is there an old monument in the middle of a new Johnson City subdivision?

Jesse Duncan is often described in the history books as the first White man to have died in Tennessee. He was attacked by Cherokee Indians near present-day Johnson City in 1765 and was buried at the site of his slaying, according to newspaper articles.

Duncan's monument, placed by local residents in 1909, currently sits in the middle of a street in Duncan's Retreat, a modern 21st-century subdivision.

A state historical marker at the corner of North Roan Street and East Mountain View Road in Johnson City marks the site of Duncan's untimely death.

The marker states: "Two and one quarter miles east, on a ridge north of the road, is the grave of this pioneer, who was killed and scalped by Indians in 1765. He was the first white man known to have been slain in this area. A monument marks the site."

A marble monument was erected in the tiny Flourville community of Washington County on September 18, 1909, according to local newspapers.

Duncan had lived with other White settlers who built a fort near the Watauga River. The Cherokee had a small town at the

JESSE DUNCAN GRAVE

WHAT: Jesse Duncan is said to be the first White man to have died in Tennessee.

WHERE: In Duncan's Retreat subdivision, Johnson City, TN 37601

COST: Free

PRO TIP: The site is near Winged Deer Park, which features an assortment of outdoor activities, plus access to Boone Lake.

A concrete obelisk stands in the center of a cul-de-sac in Johnson City, Tennessee, in honor of pioneer Jesse Duncan.

junction of the Watauga River and the Holston River (now the site of Boone Lake).

There is no written history of the incident, but tradition says that the White men of the DeVault settlement made an expedition north toward the Cherokee town. On their return to the fort, they were fired on by the Cherokee, according to a 1909 article in the *Knoxville Sentinel*.

A bullet struck Duncan. His comrades tried to save him but were compelled to flee for their safety, the newspaper said.

The first permanent settlement in Tennessee was made in 1769 on Boones Creek by William Bean. The site was a short distance from where Jesse Duncan died.

JUNALUSKA

Why is there a giant Native American statue in Johnson City?

Artist Peter Wolf Toth, who was born in Hungary, created the *Junaluska* statue. It was dedicated in front of a large crowd on November 29, 1986, at Metro-Kiwanis Park, according to an article in the *Johnson City Press*.

Toth told the crowd Junaluska was a Native American leader in the 1830s who pleaded and won the government's approval for his people to remain in the Appalachian Mountains. The tribe later became a part of the Trail of Tears, which removed Native Americans from portions of the southeastern US. Junaluska came to represent "the tribe that faced the impossible."

"When you look at the statue, I hope you don't just see another statue, but rather you see what the statue stands for," Toth said.

The dedication and the memorial's purpose further represent the changes that have occurred since the Cherokee left Tennessee.

"One hundred fifty years ago, it would've been a different situation," said Chief Robert Youngdeer,

Artist Peter Toth created at least 75 *Junaluska* statues. At least one can be found in each US state, including the one in Johnson City, Tennessee.

The Junaluska *statue and Friendship Gardens are located at Johnson City, Tennessee's, Metro-Kiwanis Park along Knob Creek Road.*

JUNALUSKA

WHAT: *Junaluska* is a historic sculpture of a Native American.

WHERE: 817 Guaranda Dr., Johnson City, TN 37604

COST: Free

PRO TIP: While here, visit the adjacent Friendship Gardens.

who represented the Cherokee in the 1980s. "We have come a long way since the Cherokee were in the Tennessee Valley."

Toth returned to Johnson City in 2018 to repair the giant statue, which is one of 74 such statues around the world. In more than 50 years, Toth has created at least one sculpture in every state, as well as in other countries.

The *Junaluska* sculpture is located in the 15-acre Metro-Kiwanis Park, which also includes softball fields, picnic shelters, a playground area, and concessions. In addition, the park features the Friendship Gardens, a three-acre special-use area used primarily for self-directed activities.

FLAG STOP ON THE TWEETSIE

Can I catch a train at the Milligan Depot?

Walkers and bikers on the Tweetsie Trail, a rails-to-trails project that links Johnson City and Elizabethton, features many bits of history, including a former Milligan University depot.

The trail opened in the summer of 2014 along the abandoned East Tennessee and Western North Carolina Railroad that stretched from Johnson City to the mountains of North Carolina. Visitors will discover several markers along the trail, including the Milligan Depot rest stop, a replica of a historic train station.

The rest stop features a shaded bench, a bike rack, and a sign detailing the history of the Milligan Depot, which was located a short distance from the college campus in rural Carter County.

On a good day, those stopping at the Milligan Depot can peer through the trees and see Milligan's beautiful Seeger Chapel.

The Tweetsie Trail, which continues to grow, is currently the longest rails-to-trails project in Tennessee and mirrors the success of the nearby Virginia Creeper Trail near Damascus.

"Milligan has a long connection with the railroad, so we're excited to once again have a presence on the Tweetsie Trail," former Milligan President Bill Greer said. "We were founded in the same year—1866—and Hardin Hall, a building on campus, was named for George Hardin, one of Milligan's first graduates and general manager of the ET & WNC Railroad."

The Tweetsie is also affectionately known as the "**E**at **T**aters and **W**ear **N**o **C**lothes" Railroad from the former line's acronym, ET&WNC (emphasis supplied).

Hikers and bicyclists often stop at the Milligan Depot while enjoying the Tweetsie Trail between Johnson City and Elizabethton in Tennessee. You can learn about the site's history on a nearby sign.

TWEETSIE TRAIL

WHAT: The Milligan Depot is a replica train station on the Tweetsie Trail.

WHERE: On the Tweetsie Trail in Elizabethton, TN 37643

COST: Free

PRO TIP: Want to ride a bike? Check out one of the bicycle rental shops in either Elizabethton or Johnson City. Shops can be found at both ends of the trail.

Professor Ted Thomas said the small depot, a flag stop, was established here by 1896. Milligan students could flag down a train at the flag stop and ride westward to Johnson City, a trip that would take 10 or 15 minutes, depending on whether one boarded at 9:20 a.m. or 3:25 p.m., according to a Milligan press release.

By 1940, passenger service ended, but freight trains continued to pass the depot. As late as 1950, Milligan's postmaster would load the college's outgoing mail in a wheelbarrow and walk to the flag stop, the release states.

The Bemberg Depot, another former Tweetsie train station, still stands on West Elk Avenue in Elizabethton.

GRANNY FEBRUARY

What are some of the legendary ghost stories in Elizabethton?

Who doesn't love a good ghost story? Head on up to Highland Cemetery in Elizabethton and you might encounter the ghost of Granny February.

The Highland Cemetery is one of the city's oldest and most historic graveyards and is the final resting place for many community leaders. It also features one of the best views overlooking downtown Elizabethton.

Local legend, however, has it that an old woman by the name of Granny February haunts the cemetery and that if you go to the graveyard at midnight on Halloween, you will hear a rocking chair moving inside a mausoleum, where people believe her remains are located.

Some say that she can be seen walking around the cemetery among the graves at night, according to *Elizabethton Star* editor Rozella Hardin. Look up Granny February online and she is mentioned on many paranormal sites. One story circulating said if you leave food at Granny February's mausoleum, she is likely to talk to you, and if the offering is particularly yummy, she will grant you a wish.

According to Hardin, legend holds that when Granny February was elderly, she suffered a seizure or a stroke. The illness

GHOST STORY

WHAT: The story of Granny February is a popular ghost story in Elizabethton.

WHERE: Highland Cemetery in Elizabethton, TN 37643

COST: Free

PRO TIP: Take a tour of Elizabethton's cemeteries. The town is home to several historic graveyards, including Highland, Green Hill, and Cedar Grove.

Take a stroll through Elizabethton, Tennessee's, Highland Cemetery, where one might encounter Granny February, who is said to have been buried inside a mausoleum.

left her in a state doctors believed was death. She was given a funeral and her casket was placed in a mausoleum.

There are several different tales about Granny February. One states that the cemetery caretaker heard the woman call for help from inside the mausoleum.

Hardin said there is nothing to actually validate that there was a real Granny February, but many people in the community still believe in her ghostly presence.

By the way, Hardin notes that you should not plan to visit the cemetery at night because it's illegal in Tennessee to visit a graveyard after sunset unless you have family buried there.

THE LABYRINTHS

Where can I walk and meditate in the Appalachian Highlands?

Unique circular paths, designed for walking meditation, can be found around the world, including in the Appalachian Highlands.

A labyrinth has only one path that leads from the outer edge in a circuitous way to the center, according to Veriditas, a nonprofit organization that supports labyrinth facilitators. There are no tricks and no dead ends. Unlike a maze where you might lose your way, the labyrinth is a spiritual tool that can help you find your way.

Several churches, and even private property owners, have developed labyrinths, including First Presbyterian Church in Elizabethton, Tennessee.

Volunteers at the church installed one in 2009. The design was based on a classical model that dates back almost 3,500 years. A Peace Pole, a unique landmark designed to spread peace around the world, was later installed in 2010.

First Presbyterian advises guests to pause at the entrance of the labyrinth to take a few breaths and let go of expectations and internal chatter. Go at your own pace and be respectful of others on the path.

Pay attention to your body messages, what you are sensing, or memories that come as you walk, according to a church brochure. This action is the releasing part of your journey.

Stay in the center as long as you like. When you are ready to leave, just follow the same path out.

St. John's Episcopal Church in Johnson City, Tennessee, has an indoor labyrinth that is open to the public. Just contact the church to make sure it is available. It was modeled after one at Chartres Cathedral in France. It is beautifully hand-painted on canvas and measures 30 feet in diameter, according to the church website.

Labyrinths can be found around the region, including one at First Presbyterian Church in Elizabethton, Tennessee.

In Abingdon, Virginia, guests are welcome to visit a privately owned labyrinth, also designed after the Chartres labyrinth, at 250 Valley Street. Park across the street or walk from nearby Plumb Alley.

Other labyrinths can be found at Greeneville Middle School; St. Mary's Catholic Church in Johnson City; St. Christopher's Episcopal Church in Kingsport; Jubilee House Retreat Center in Abingdon; a private property at 20449 Alvarado Road in Abingdon; and Emmanuel Episcopal Church in Bristol, Virginia.

LABYRINTHS OF THE APPALACHIAN HIGHLANDS

WHAT: Several private and public labyrinths can be found around the Appalachian Highlands region.

WHERE: Several locations, including First Presbyterian Church in Elizabethton, TN; Greeneville Middle School; St. Christopher's Episcopal Church in Kingsport, TN; and 205 Valley St. in Abingdon, VA.

COST: Free

PRO TIP: Keep your distance from other people who are there to meditate and don't wish to feel crowded.

GIDDYAP! BETSY'S UPPING STONES

What are those random concrete steps along the road?

Hidden treasures can be found throughout historic downtown Elizabethton—including a couple obscure upping stones.

What's an upping stone? It is a permanently emplaced stone block used to step up to a horse-drawn carriage to gain entry or exit from it. Before residents hit the streets with their motorized automobiles, they either walked, went by horseback, or if they had the luxury, would ride in a horse-drawn carriage.

In order to enter or exit a high-ground-clearance carriage, residents would install concrete steps in front of their homes, businesses, and churches. These upping stones are also known as carriage blocks and hitching posts.

While driving around town, at first glance, you may think they look like some displaced steps. But at least two intentionally placed upping stones can be found today in Elizabethton.

One such stone was installed at the home of Capt. L.H. Rhudy, who lived near the Elizabethton Covered Bridge. Rhudy's home, built in 1894, is located on Hattie Avenue. He was a businessman and industrialist and assisted in the development of downtown Elizabethton.

STEPPING STONES

WHAT: Historic Elizabethton is home to a few upping stones, which were used when horses and buggies were the prevalent means of transportation.

WHERE: 600 block of Hattie Ave., Elizabethton, TN 37643

COST: Free

PRO TIP: You can't miss the nearby historic Elizabethton Covered Bridge, the most photographed landmark in the state of Tennessee, or the antique 1921 Model T fire engine on Hattie.

A historic stepping stone sits in the front yard of an Elizabethton, Tennessee, residence, not far from the historic covered bridge.

The brick home features a perfectly maintained concrete upping stone. It comes with a hitching ring so residents could tie up their horses while visiting the home.

The second upping stone sits in front of the Alfred Moore Carter Mansion in the 800 block of East Elk Avenue near the county courthouse. This Greek Revival house was constructed in 1819 and is named for Alfred Moore Carter, the son of Carter County's namesake, Landon Carter, and Elizabethton's namesake, Elizabeth Carter.

Other historic upping stones can be found in Jonesborough and Kingsport, Tennessee.

NOT YOUR ORDINARY LIBRARY

What's so strange about this public library?

The Elizabethton–Carter County Public Library is housed in a beautiful former post office building—one which the government also used as a safehouse for the event of a nuclear war. Peer inside the building, which is listed on the National Register of Historic Places, and discover an array of unique features.

The Beaux Arts building was constructed in downtown Elizabethton in 1932 and has a raised ashlar basement, according to the National Register. The building's facade features eight Ionic columns. The NRHP describes the architecture as very unique for the area and one of the best examples of Beaux Arts.

Postal service employees began occupying the building in 1933. The federal government owned the property until the late 1980s, when a new post office opened on West Elk Avenue.

The city of Elizabethton renovated the structure and eventually opened its new library in the building in 1992. The library was previously located across the street from the present-day library.

The original library also housed a Cold War–era fallout shelter. The Office of Civil Defense launched the National Shelter

---

The National Shelter Program sponsored a few fallout shelters in the Appalachian Highlands, including the Elizabethton, Tennessee, library; the Veterans of Foreign Wars post in Elizabethton; the post office in Kingsport, Tennessee; and Shoemaker Elementary School in Gate City, Virginia.

The Elizabethton–Carter County Public Library originally served as the community's post office, as well as a nuclear fallout shelter.

POST LIBRARY

WHAT: The Elizabethton, Tennessee, public library is located in a former post office and features an old fallout shelter.

WHERE: 201 N Sycamore St., Elizabethton, TN 37643

COST: Free

PRO TIP: The library is home to Elizabethton's archives, which features great historic documents, records, and photographs, as well as a microfilm reader.

Program in 1962 and located such buildings where residents could seek protection from potential nuclear elements. A fallout shelter sign could be seen at one time on the outside of the building, but it was apparently stolen by a thief and has not been seen since.

"There are many elements of the old post office still visible here at the library," said Elizabethton archivist Joseph Penza.

Loading docks from the post office are still standing, and there is a "POSTMASTER" door in the main library as well as a catwalk that had been used to monitor thieves, Penza said.

LIFE'S A BEACH IN THE MOUNTAINS

Where are there beaches in the Appalachian Highlands?

The Appalachian Highlands is known for its breathtaking mountain scenery, so many visitors might be surprised to learn it is also home to several beautiful beaches.

Local residents often spend their summers at the lake, sunbathing on the beach, and enjoying the cool serene waters. There are several sandy beaches at area lakes, both natural and man-made.

One of the most popular beaches can be found at Watauga Lake in Carter County. The Shook Branch Recreation Area is located on the southern shore of the Tennessee Valley Authority reservoir. The 20-acre site includes a large, grassy area for picnicking, picnic tables with grills, and a designated swimming beach.

Another beach can be found on South Holston Lake at the remote Jacob's Creek Recreation Area. This beach, which includes a campground, is spread over a peninsula on the eastern side of the lake in the Cherokee National Forest.

After hitting the beach at Jacob's Creek, be sure to stretch your legs on the shoreside trail.

In Virginia, head on over to historic Hungry Mother State Park, one of the state's original six parks. It features a 108-acre lake in the heart of the mountains. The park's sandy beach features a bathhouse, boat rentals, a boat launch, and an accessible fishing pier.

Want to spend the night at Hungry Mother? Check out one of the park's yurts, a unique round tent. The furnished yurts at Virginia State Parks are modern versions of traditional structures. They offer the halfway point between tent camping and staying in a full-service cabin, according to Virginia State Parks.

A lifeguard tower sits on the beach at Hungry Mother State Park in Southwest Virginia. Photo courtesy of Virginia Department of Conservation and Recreation.

Other beaches in the Appalachian Highlands can be found at the High Knob Lake near Norton, Virginia, and Boone Lake beach near the Boone Dam in Tennessee.

GO TO THE BEACH

WHAT: Several lakeshore beaches can be found around the Appalachian Highlands region.

WHERE: Watauga Lake, South Holston Lake, Boone Lake, Hungry Mother State Park, and others

COST: Varies depending on location

PRO TIP: If you're looking for a quieter beach, check out the Jacob's Creek Recreation Area, which also features a campground.

GHOST CHOIR

What is the mysterious music that some say can be heard on Roan Mountain?

One of the Appalachian Highlands' most unusual and mesmerizing mysteries is the century-old story of the Ghostly Choir of Roan Mountain.

The story is often shared by those who have ventured onto the mountain, but the cause has never been determined.

Fred Behrend, a former editor at the *Elizabethton Star*, spent much of his free time on the 6,285-foot-high Roan Mountain. He loved to tell tales of the noises, which have also been called either the Devil's Choir of Roan Mountain or the Angels of Roan Mountain, depending on who experienced them.

Editor Rozella Hardin, a local historian, also enjoys retelling the legend of the ghostly music that has been heard on Roan Mountain since long before White settlers have been in the county. The Catawba tribe was said to challenge the other tribes in the area to battles that were so bloody and gory that they caused the rhododendron on the edge of the Roan Bald to bloom red.

What does the music sound like? That's also disputed. Some people claim it's the sound of angels rehearsing their songs for the end of time. Some believe that the song is merely the rushing sound of a natural wind, magnified by the configuration of rocks on Roan Mountain. However, the wind on Roan Mountain seems

GHOST CHOIR OF ROAN MOUNTAIN

WHAT: Mysterious sounds have been heard on Roan Mountain for centuries.

WHERE: Off Tennessee State Route 143, Roan Mountain, TN 37687

COST: Free

PRO TIP: Take a hike on the Cloudland Trail for some spectacular scenery.

The former Cloudland Hotel is in the background of the left photograph, which is courtesy of the Library of Congress. The right photograph features Roan Mountain's rhododendron gardens.

to be anything but normal because other people have said that the sound is horrible and resembles an animal howling.

One legend has it that a brave soul set out to find the origin of the music, only to fall and be knocked out, Hardin said. During this time, the boy dreamed of a horrid choir of ghosts, ghouls, and demons floating in the air singing to him.

Guests of the former Cloudland Hotel, a late 19th-century resort that was located on Roan Mountain, reported, "The wind's song was said to be louder than a thousand humming bees encircling your head."

The cause remains unknown.

"Whatever the source of the music, it can still be heard after a storm," wrote Behrend in one of his columns. Behrend shared that some claimed the music was accompanied by a circular rainbow.

The rhododendron gardens are in full bloom and the Rhododendron Festival is held in mid-June on Roan Mountain, a great time to visit and listen to the Ghost Choir.

UNCLE NICK

Where is hermit Nick Grindstaff buried?

One of the world's most famous—yet private—hermits lived atop Iron Mountain in Northeast Tennessee during the early 20th century. Nick Grindstaff's grave site and monument are located adjacent to the Appalachian Trail and are visited by thousands of hikers every year as they pass through the area.

The inscription on Grindstaff's monument says he "lived alone, suffered alone, and died alone." The hermit's grave is located along the Carter County and Johnson County border and is about 13 miles from Watauga Lake.

Grindstaff, known by many as Uncle Nick, was the son of Isaac Grindstaff and Mary Heaton. He was born December 26, 1851. He was orphaned at a young age, and he and his siblings were raised by relatives. As a young man, Grindstaff is said to have sold his share of his family's property and gone west to seek his fortune.

Eventually, Grindstaff returned to Tennessee, but *why* is another question. There are several stories about what happened

NICK GRINDSTAFF'S GRAVE

WHAT: Known hermit Nick Grindstaff is buried atop Iron Mountain.

WHERE: Appalachian Trail south of Tennessee State Route 91, Shady Valley, TN 37688

COST: Free

PRO TIP: This one requires an approximately seven-mile round trip hike on the Appalachian Trail from Tennessee State Route 91.

Nick Grindstaff's remote grave site can be reached on the Appalachian Trail from either State Route 91 or Wilbur Dam Road.

Nick Grindstaff's monument is often shrouded in Iron Mountain fog. The hermit's grave is along the Appalachian Trail. Photo courtesy of Lisa Germaine.

out West. He may have been beaten and robbed. His wife may have tragically died. Nonetheless, he was traumatized and decided to return to Tennessee by himself, where he settled on Iron Mountain.

He lived on the mountain alone for more than 40 years. He built a home and fences, cleared land, and gathered roots and herbs to trade in the valley.

The hermit died on July 22, 1923. A friend found him in his bed one day. His dog, Panter, guarded the body. Local men then buried Grindstaff on the mountain near his home. Newspapers reported that dozens of local residents, many who had never met him, attended his funeral.

His remote grave site and monument can be reached along the Appalachian Trail, either northbound from the Wilbur Dam Road crossing or southbound from the State Route 91 crossing. Panter is buried next to Grindstaff.

OLD CHURCH

Where's the oldest church in Tennessee?

Tennessee's oldest church still in existence at its original location can be found along the Old Elizabethton Highway between Johnson City and Elizabethton. Located in what is now Carter County, Sinking Creek Baptist Church was organized in 1772—when the area was still Washington County.

The church is named for a tributary of the Watauga River that passes through the eastern side of Johnson City.

The Sinking Creek congregation had some troubles early on, according to news articles. Records indicate that the problems stemmed from Indian raids in 1776, which caused church services to be discontinued for a while.

Later, after the threat of Indian uprisings died down, Matthew Talbot reorganized the church and served as its pastor. Talbot owned a large farm where Sycamore Shoals State Park is now located.

Worship services continued throughout the years, except during the Civil War from 1861 to 1865, according to the church records.

In 1778, evangelists Charles and John Chastain, brothers from Virginia, held a revival in the area, and the need for a larger church was realized. Church leaders planned and erected what is now known as the Old Log Church, which still stands on the property.

SINKING CREEK BAPTIST CHURCH

WHAT: Sinking Creek Baptist Church is recognized as the oldest church still in existence in Tennessee.

WHERE: 2313 Elizabethton Hwy., Johnson City, TN 37601

COST: Free

PRO TIP: If you want to see the inside of the church, call ahead at 423-928-3222.

The congregation at Sinking Creek Baptist Church in Carter County, Tennessee, restored the historic log facility in 2023.

A larger brick church was constructed adjacent to the log church in 1962.

The log church, which features wooden seats, remains a landmark of the Sinking Creek community. Restoration work began on the church in 2022.

A new brick facility was built at Sinking Creek in 1962, the same time E. Reece Harris began serving as the longest-standing pastor. He served until 2012.

SHADY VALLEY'S TREASURES

A big chair on the snake? Huh?

The Shady Valley Country Store is located along the 112-mile Snake, a popular motorcycle route that zigzags through the mountains and Backbone Rock.

Out front, visitors will find a big yellow chair, a perfect spot to take a selfie or a family photo. Enjoy a cheeseburger and a soft drink, and rest on one of the rockers or the Big Yellow Chair.

The store is located at the corner of US Highway 421 and Tennessee State Route 133 in the community of Shady Valley. Founded in the 1920s and moved to its present location in 1948, the country store is the epicenter of motorcycling in Northeast Tennessee and is often used as a rest stop for motorcyclists.

Well known locally, the Snake is often considered one of the best-kept-secret motorcycle and sports car routes in Tennessee, crossing three mountains. The 37-mile portion of Highway 421 between Sullivan County and Johnson County is the most popular section of the route. It contains 489 curves and crosses South Holston Lake and the Appalachian Trail.

While Snake 421 is the most popular route, many motorcyclists also take the round trip via Tennessee Route 91 and Tennessee Route 133. That connection takes riders through Mountain City, Damascus, and Backbone Rock.

The railroad tracks through Backbone Rock were taken up in 1924 and the route was opened for automobiles, which continue to pass through the tunnel today.

Motorcyclists can also check out the Back of the Dragon in Southwest Virginia.

A portion of the Snake zips through Backbone Rock Recreation Area, a must-see in northern Johnson County along Route 133. A tunnel was drilled through the rock in 1901 to allow railroad access between Shady Valley and Damascus. Drivers today pass through what is known as "The Shortest Tunnel in the World" as they travel along Route 133.

BACKBONE ROCK AND THE SNAKE

WHAT: The Snake motorcycle route takes visitors across the mountains of Northeast Tennessee.

WHERE: The route follows US Hwy. 421 and Tennessee State Route 133 east of Bristol.

COST: Free

PRO TIP: This highway passes by some great spots for photos, such as Backbone Rock on Tennessee State Route 133.

The Big Chair sits outside of the Shady Valley Country Store at the corner of US Highway 421 and State Route 133.

TENNESSEE'S STATE SONG

Where is the real Copperhead Road?

There's a good chance you'll go to visit the legendary Copperhead Road near Mountain City and the sign won't be there. Ever since country rock singer and songwriter Steve Earle released "Copperhead Road" in 1988, the street signs have become souvenirs for thieves.

The song, which topped the charts in both 1988 and again in 2021 due to online downloads, tells the story of a Vietnam War veteran named John Lee Pettimore, a descendent of a moonshine bootlegging clan.

Earle sings: "Same as my daddy and his daddy before / You hardly ever saw grandaddy down here / He only came to town about twice a year / He'd buy a hundred pounds of yeast and some copper line / Everybody knew that he made moonshine."

The "revenue man," a term used for law enforcement who sought those involved in the illegal manufacturing and distribution of moonshine, was looking for "grandaddy," Earle sings.

Pettimore's father drove a "big block Dodge," which had the phrase "Johnson County Sheriff" painted on the side, and ran moonshine to Knoxville with a weekly load. Earle sings, "You could smell the whiskey burnin' down Copperhead Road."

Today, visitors might not smell burning whiskey but they may discover some delightful wines. The area near Watauga Lake, where

---

With the most recent additions of "Copperhead Road" and "The Tennessee in Me" from the film *Country Strong* in 2023, Tennessee has 12 state songs, the most in the country.

The sign is missing from Copperhead Hollow Road, the namesake of Steve Earle's "Copperhead Road." The road is located in rural Johnson County, Tennessee.

Copperhead Road is located, is home to a few wineries, including one near the legendary road named for the picturesque lake.

Copperhead Road, which was changed to Copperhead Hollow Road due to its infamous history, has gained recent fame after the Tennessee legislature named "Copperhead Road" the 11th state song. It joins other songs such as "Rocky Top" and "Tennessee Waltz."

But Earle notes in his song that once Pettimore began planting marijuana, "You better stay away from Copperhead Road."

COPPERHEAD ROAD

WHAT: The road memorialized in Tennessee's state song is real and it's located in Johnson County.

WHERE: Copperhead Hollow Rd., Mountain City, TN 37683

COST: Free (Unless you take the sign and then it's a fine and conviction for theft.)

PRO TIP: Copperhead Road is now known as Copperhead Hollow Road and is located near some of the region's best wineries such as Watauga Lake Winery and Villa Nove Vineyards.

BUTLER MUSEUM

Where can I learn more about the town that wouldn't drown?

Many have heard the story of Butler, the Tennessee town that wouldn't drown, but did you know you can see some of the artifacts from the old town at an often overlooked museum?

The Butler Museum, which can be found in the relocated town of Butler, features some unique artifacts, like a horse-drawn hearse and a reconstruction of the former post office. The museum is located at the end of McQueen Street, a thoroughfare that didn't exist when the Tennessee Valley Authority built the Watauga Dam.

The old town of Butler was flooded in 1948 after the construction of Watauga Dam. The TVA had bought out the town and moved about 40 homes to higher ground. The new town, also known as Butler, is located just north of Watauga Lake, the reservoir created by the new dam.

Before the water inundated Butler, residents saved many artifacts, including the horse drawn hearse, the interior of the post office, a stained-glass window from the old Methodist church, showcases from some of Butler's stores, and equipment from the old lumber mill.

The Butler Museum originally opened in 2000 and features many of these artifacts, as well as displays about Butler's unique history. It tells the story of the deadly floods that had affected the community in the early 20th century causing the

BUTLER MUSEUM

WHAT: Learn about "the town that wouldn't drown" at the Butler Museum.

WHERE: 123 Selma Curtis Rd., Butler, TN 37640

COST: $5 per adult

PRO TIP: The museum is open from Memorial Day weekend to October, and also hosts Old Butler Day each August.

The Butler Museum in rural Johnson County, Tennessee, features a variety of artifacts from Old Butler, which was lost when the Tennessee Valley Authority constructed the Watauga Dam. Photo courtesy of the Butler Museum.

federal government to build the dam. The exhibit includes many photographs and artifacts that describe life in Butler before, during, and after dam construction.

The museum, built in the style of the old Butler train station, also includes a reconstructed Bluebird Team Room.

A drawdown of Watauga Lake in 1983 allowed former residents to visit the exposed remains of old Butler.

FIDDLERS' CONVENTION

What's the story on the murals in downtown Mountain City?

The legendary Mountain City Fiddlers' Convention was first held in Johnson County in May of 1925. Its musicians helped to define the music of East Tennessee. Along with the Bristol recording sessions of 1927 and the Johnson City sessions of 1928 and 1929, the Mountain City event is regarded as one of the defining moments in the launching of the country music industry.

Several beautifully crafted murals can be found along downtown Mountain City's Mural Trail. Each depicts an aspect of Mountain City's contribution to early country music, including the fiddlers' convention.

The fiddlers' convention is depicted in a large mural at 127 College Street, on the Johnson County Center for the Arts building, and was painted by about 20 community members of all ages. The event was held nearby at the Old High School, now known as Heritage Hall. The crowd was so large they were afraid the floor would cave in. As a result, the nearby courthouse and elementary school were opened to the public to house the overflow crowd.

Several successful musicians were inspired by the convention to begin

The fiddlers' convention continues to be held in downtown Mountain City, including one in 2023, which was hosted by local Kody Norris.

The fiddlers' convention mural is painted on the back of the Johnson County Center for the Arts building in Mountain City, Tennessee.

their recording careers, including Clarence "Tom" Ashley, Bertie Jenkins, Walt Bacon, Argil Bowman, Uncle "Am" Stuart, John Rector, Fiddlin' John Carson, Al Hopkins, Fiddlin' Powers, G. B. Grayson, and Henry Whitter.

Other murals in downtown Mountain City include *Birth of a Ballad*, which tells the story of Tom Dooley, an infamous outlaw who was captured in Johnson County. Grayson, one of the musicians inspired by the convention, recorded the earliest version of "The Ballad of Tom Dooley" back in 1929. The Dooley mural is located at 101 Old South Church Street.

FIDDLERS' CONVENTION

WHAT: Take a walk around downtown Mountain City to view some of the town's murals, including one that depicts the fiddlers' convention.

WHERE: Downtown Mountain City, TN 37683

COST: Free

PRO TIP: There are plenty of other things to see in Mountain City, including the fire tower on Doe Mountain and the antique shops on Main Street.

SCARY TUNNEL

Why is Sensabaugh Tunnel one of the scariest places in the Appalachian Highlands?

The Sensabaugh Tunnel in Hawkins County, Tennessee, is considered a nationally recognized urban legend, according to the city of Kingsport.

Built in the 1920s and named after Edward Sensabaugh, who owned the land on which the tunnel was built, this landmark is filled with history and legend. The 12-foot-high tunnel, which is about 380 feet long, is paved and located in Hawkins County but sits near the city of Kingsport and the North Fork of the Holston River.

There have been many tales including murder, satanic rituals, and hauntings shared over the years about the legendary tunnel.

In one story, Sensabaugh is said to have let a homeless man into his home, but his guest decided to try to steal jewelry. As the story goes, when Sensabaugh confronted the man with a gun, the homeless man grabbed their baby daughter and used her as a shield.

The man got away but drowned the baby in the tunnel. Ponding on the roadway has been called a Crybaby Pool, and people often report that they have heard a crying baby in the tunnel.

Another story said Sensabaugh went mad and killed his entire family, throwing their bodies into the tunnel.

SENSABAUGH TUNNEL

WHAT: Sensabaugh Tunnel is featured in several guides to scary sites and ghost stories.

WHERE: On Sensabaugh Hollow Rd., Church Hill, TN 37642

COST: Free

PRO TIP: Bring your imagination when visiting the tunnel, and visit at dusk, if you dare.

Vehicles can still pass through the old Sensabaugh Tunnel, which local residents believe is haunted. It is located on Sensabaugh Hollow Road.

In a third story, Sensabaugh grows old and vandals and teens begin taking over the tunnel for fun. Sensabaugh would then hide at one end of the tunnel and fill it with an eerie shriek, scaring anyone lurking inside, the city officials said.

Want to experience the horrors of Sensabaugh Tunnel? Here's what you might expect: if you switch off your car engine in the middle of the tunnel, it won't switch back on. In addition to hearing the crying baby, one can also hear approaching footsteps—supposedly those of Sensabaugh. Some say the shadow of a woman may also appear in your back seat.

DON'T STOP THE PRESS!

Where can I learn about newspapers published in Tennessee?

The first newspaper published in Tennessee was printed in 1791 in the small town of Rogersville. More than 200 years later, you can learn about it at the Tennessee Newspaper and Printing Museum, which is located in an old railroad depot.

George Roulstone, who published the first Tennessee newspaper, originally worked in Fayetteville, North Carolina, where he packed up his printing equipment and journeyed across the mountains by horse and wagon.

Roulstone ended up in Rogersville, where he published the *Knoxville Gazette*, which has been described as the first piece of printing ever attempted in Tennessee.

The newspaper man and his partner, Robert Ferguson, worked in Rogersville until 1792.

Scroll forward a couple of centuries: a newspaper museum opened in Rogersville in 2002 and features Roulstone's 1791 newspaper.

The museum also features the contents of three other printshops from the region, dating back to the late 19th and early 20th centuries, according to the Rogersville Heritage Association, which manages the attraction.

All of the essential print shop equipment, such as a large paper cutter, type cabinets, worktables, wire stitches, and proof presses are also on display, the heritage association says on its website.

The last linotype machine ever to be used to set type for a newspaper in Tennessee, which came from the *Rogersville Review*, is on display at the museum. The linotype machine was used until 1982.

Old newspaper equipment from across Tennessee is on display at the Tennessee Newspaper and Printing Museum in Hawkins County. Photos courtesy of Rogersville Heritage Association.

NEWSPAPER MUSEUM

WHAT: Learn about the newspaper industry at the Tennessee Newspaper and Printing Museum in Rogersville.

WHERE: 415 S Depot St., Rogersville, TN 37857

COST: Free, but donations accepted

PRO TIP: The gem of this museum is the last linotype machine ever to be used to set type for a Tennessee newspaper.

Tennessee organizations, including the McClung Historical Collection in Knoxville, donated newspapers and press equipment when Rogersville's newspaper museum first opened.

Little did Roulstone and Ferguson know that Rogersville would be just 15 miles from the future site of Pressman's Home, established in 1889. The International Pressman and Assistants' Union was housed at Pressman's Home, an obscure, abandoned attraction in Hawkins County.

THE RIVER

What parts of *The River* were filmed here?

Hollywood has visited the Appalachian Highlands on many occasions over the years, and it has left a special mark on a recreation area in Hawkins County.

Set along the Holston River, the 440-acre Laurel Run Park served as the backdrop for the 1984 movie *The River*, which starred Mel Gibson and Sissy Spacek.

The River is about a farming family that endured severe storms, threats by the bank to repossess their farm, and other hard times in a battle to save their land.

After the conclusion of the movie, the property was ceded to Hawkins County. The county then began the journey to turn the rugged farmland along the beautiful and serene Holston River into a community park.

The park features an array of wildlife, including deer, rabbits, opossums, turkeys, turtles, frogs, otters, beavers, hawks, coyotes, and even an occasional bear. It also has approximately one-half mile of river frontage where you can fish for catfish and bass (largemouth, smallmouth, and red eye), according to the Hawkins County Parks Department.

Inside the park is a one-mile paved walking trail along the river's edge, as well as athletic fields and multiple picnic shelters.

In addition, there are 37.5 miles of trails in conjunction with nearby Bays Mountain Park, which includes a trail to Laurel Falls.

Several movies have been filmed in the Appalachian Highlands region, including *The River*, *Big Stone Gap*, and *Days of Thunder*, which includes a scene at Bristol Motor Speedway.

The film The River *is set along the Holston River near Church Hill, Tennessee. The filming site is now a public park.*

Scenes from *The River* were also filmed in downtown Gate City, Virginia.

LAUREL RUN PARK

WHAT: Scenes from *The River* were filmed at Laurel Run Park in Hawkins County.

WHERE: 364 Laurel Run Park Rd., Church Hill, TN 37642

COST: Free

PRO TIP: Two waterfalls are accessible from Laurel Run Park, including Laurel Falls and Kiner Creek Falls.

FISH HATCHERY

Where can I see the production of fish eggs and a collection of fine dishware in one trip?

More than 16 million trout fish eggs are produced each year at Erwin's National Fish Hatchery, which is also home to the Unicoi County Heritage Museum's collection of locally made glass and pottery.

Guests are welcome to visit the fish hatchery, which was established in 1897 by what would become the US Fish and Wildlife Service. The site produces millions of trout eggs for federal, state, tribal, university, and research centers. During the early days of operation, the eggs were transported by train "fish cars," where fish culturists would manually aerate the water and add more ice as needed along the route, according to the hatchery brochures. Today, the eggs are transported by FedEx and other delivery companies.

In addition to self-guided tours and feeding the fish, visitors can hike the nature trail, picnic, and observe spawning processes, pollinator gardens, beehives, and more.

In 1903, officials built a grand home for the hatchery's superintendent. But by 1982, the old house had become dilapidated, and the federal government ordered its demolition. Local residents, however, had a different

ERWIN NATIONAL FISH HATCHERY

WHAT: Learn about fish production and local fine dishware in Erwin.

WHERE: 520 Federal Hatchery Rd., Erwin, TN 37650

COST: Grounds of fish hatchery are free. Admission to the Unicoi County Heritage Museum and Clinchfield Railroad Museum is $4 per adult.

PRO TIP: In addition to the fish hatchery and museums, the site also features a leisurely natural trail worth visiting.

Trout fish production can be observed at Erwin, Tennessee's, National Fish Hatchery, which is also home to the county's history museum.

idea. The superintendent's house was transitioned into the Unicoi County Heritage Museum.

The house features the following themed rooms: Parlor, Blue Ridge Pottery Room, Butler's Pantry, Community Room, Wildlife Room, Kitchen, Main Street, Clinchfield Railroad Room, Daughters of the American Revolution Room, History and War Rooms, Attic, Country Store, Greasy Cove Schoolhouse, and Amphitheatre.

The museum's collection of locally made dishware is one of the best and largest in the region. For decades, Erwin was home to several pottery and glassware manufacturers, including Southern Potteries and Cash Family Pottery. They employed thousands of people from the area and, along with the railroad, contributed much to Erwin's growth in the 20th century.

Erwin is home to two unique fish hatcheries, one operated by the state of Tennessee, and another by the federal government.

A HORSE, OF COURSE!

What's in the basement at the Unicoi County library?

The staff of the library in Erwin, Tennessee, have a secret. They are hiding a horse in the basement of their historic building.

During the late 1990s, crews began renovating the former Clinchfield railroad depot in Erwin to make it into a library. While working in the basement, they uncovered a horse.

Do not worry; the horse is not real. It is either a carving into the brick foundation or a plaster cast of a horse.

HORSE CARVING

WHAT: A horse was found carved into a wall at the Unicoi County Public Library in 2000.

WHERE: 201 Nolichucky Ave., Erwin, TN 37650

COST: Free

PRO TIP: Want to see the horse? Just ask library staff and they will be happy to show you.

After its discovery, historic preservation officials recommended that the horse, which can be found in a dark corner of the library, be covered and protected.

The horse is now encased behind a wood-and-glass frame.

The station was constructed in 1925. Before then, railroad crews worked in a boxcar in Erwin. Kenneth Toney, the grandson of the late Col. J. Frank Toney,

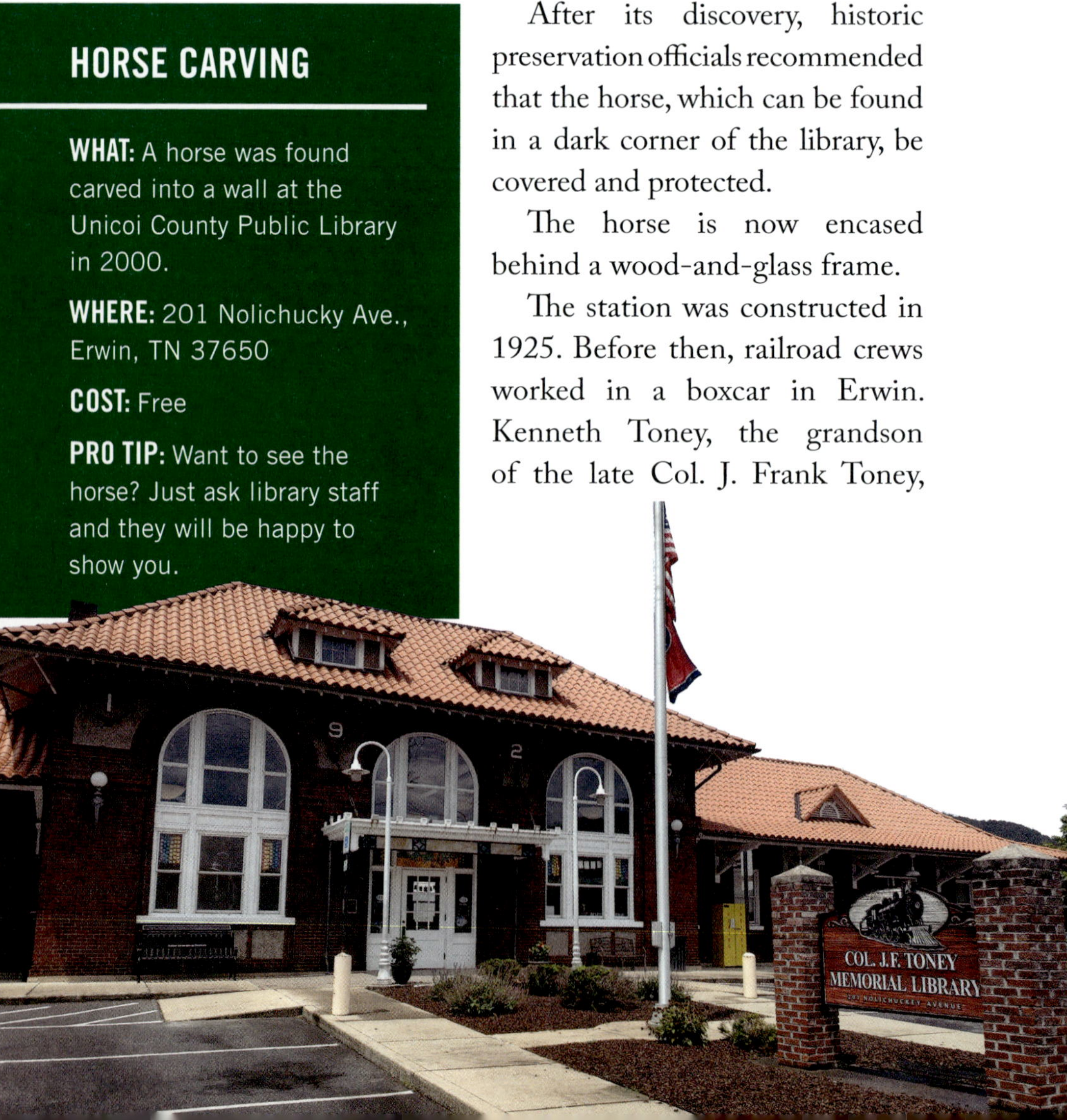

A horse, likely created by a railroad worker in the 1920s, is on display in the basement of the Unicoi County Library in Erwin, Tennessee.

purchased the property in 1989 and donated it to the town for the purpose of establishing a library.

The library was later dedicated in January 1999 following renovations. It was during those renovations that crews found the horse.

Historians in Erwin believe the horse was carved by a railroad worker or a construction worker during the station's original construction in the 1920s.

"Whoever did it, did have some talent," architect Ron Jones told the *Erwin Record* in 2000.

GRISLY ELEPHANT STORY

Where, why, and how did Mary the elephant die?

In September 1916, a circus elephant named Mary was hanged from a Clinchfield Railroad derrick in the small town of Erwin, Tennessee.

Mary died in Erwin and is likely to have been buried somewhere near the railroad, after newspapers reported that she killed a trainer about 35 miles away in Kingsport. She was part of the Sparks Circus, which was making its way around Appalachia.

There are numerous versions of the story of what happened, but Mary is believed to have been spooked before killing the trainer. Some say she threw him and crushed him in front of a crowd of shocked onlookers.

A man shot Mary multiple times but the bullets didn't injure her. She was then sentenced to death by the elephant's owner.

Mary, a five-ton elephant, was taken to Erwin, a small nearby town with a large rail yard and a derrick big enough to hang an elephant. Thousands of people watched Mary hang from the derrick.

MARY THE ELEPHANT

WHAT: Mary, a circus elephant, was hanged in the railroad yard at Erwin in 1916.

WHERE: Downtown Erwin, TN 37650

COST: Free

PRO TIP: The railroad company frowns upon people entering the rail yard to look for Mary relics.

The story of Mary the elephant's death has been depicted in countless pieces of art, including music, plays, and books.

Mary the elephant was hung and likely buried in the rail yard in Erwin, Tennessee, which is pictured here from Second Street.

It's unknown exactly where Mary was buried, but she is believed to have been laid to rest in the rail yard. The incident quickly led to Erwin being known as the town that hung an elephant.

Mary's legacy lives on today, primarily through preserved newspaper articles and art. The Unicoi County Heritage Museum features several newspaper clippings of the event.

Elephant statue figures have been scattered across Erwin in recent years, including a nine-foot-tall statue along Main Avenue in downtown. The pachyderm sculpture, created by the owner of Backyard Terrors Dinosaur Park, was installed in 2016 but has since been moved.

Several smaller fiberglass elephants have also been on display in town. Through RISE: Erwin, an organization that was created to help the town embrace its history, the elephants were put on the auction block to raise money.

GHOST TOWN

Where is the Lost Cove community?

The Lost Cove community, which sits on the border between Tennessee and North Carolina, was once a thriving town. It has, however, since become an obscure ghost town in the mountains.

Historian Pat Alderman describes Lost Cove as "one of eastern America's most legendary ghost towns," which had developed in the late 19th century as a self-sustaining remote mountain community.

Lost Cove has always been physically isolated, according to historian and author Christy Smith. It lies at the edge of Unicoi County, Tennessee, and Mitchell and Yancey Counties in North Carolina. The cove sits along the Nolichucky River where it crosses through the gorge.

No roads have ever reached Lost Cove. Today, the very few visitors that go there must travel on foot, either via Lost Cove Trail 196 from Yancey County or by taking a hike along the railroad tracks from Unicoi County at River Road.

One must take a long hike into the woods to discover the abandoned buildings in the old Lost Cove community. Photos courtesy of Southern Appalachian Highlands Conservancy.

LOST COVE COMMUNITY

WHAT: The former Lost Cove community is a ghost town along the Tennessee and North Carolina border.

WHERE: Lost Cove on Tennessee and North Carolina state line

COST: Free

PRO TIP: The town can be reached from both Unicoi County in Tennessee and Yancey County in North Carolina.

Lost Cove covers about 400 acres, according to Smith. The community was established sometime around the Civil War and lasted through the early 20th century. The residents farmed and made moonshine, Smith said.

Smith believes the community's dependence on the outside world in the early 20th century is what led to its death. The railroad and timber industries may have dealt the final blow to Lost Cove because when those industries began to prosper, Lost Cove became defunct.

The last family moved out of Lost Cove in 1957. Today, visitors will only find abandoned buildings, such as a church and some empty homes.

THE LOST STATE

Have you ever heard of the lost state of Franklin?

For approximately four years in the late 1700s, the people of Northeast Tennessee briefly joined the short-lived state of Franklin. The residents named the state in honor of Benjamin Franklin, a polymath, or person of wide-ranging knowledge. Franklin, however, never supported the state, which only lasted from 1784 to 1788.

There are several artifacts that remain today as proof of the existence of the lost state, including a reconstructed log capitol building in Greeneville. State of Franklin Road is one of the busiest thoroughfares in Johnson City, and several businesses and organizations still use the name State of Franklin.

Following the Revolutionary War, the state of Franklin's first general assembly met in 1785 and elected John Sevier as governor. Many in the region supported the state due to the region's isolation from North Carolina across the Appalachian Mountains. North Carolina, however, wanted to maintain control of the land, which led the federal government not to accept Franklin as a state. As a result, two governments, Franklin and North Carolina, simultaneously controlled the region of Northeast Tennessee.

The Franklin Legislature, which met at the capitol building, challenged the authority of North Carolina by passing laws to levy taxes, raise a militia, establish courts, authorize the performance of marriages, and open a land office, according to a historic marker in Greeneville.

Today, the replica of the state of Franklin's capitol building features wood benches, a counter, and a map showing counties within the forgotten state.

A replica of the state of Franklin's capitol building is located between College and Main Streets in downtown Greeneville, Tennessee.

STATE OF FRANKLIN

WHAT: Greeneville, Tennessee, once served as the capital of the state of Franklin.

WHERE: 208 N College St., Greeneville, TN 37745

COST: Free

PRO TIP: Learn more about downtown Greeneville with the 90-minute "A Walk with the President" guided tour, which is available through Main Street Greeneville Tours.

Eventually, in 1788, the state of North Carolina ceded its lands west of the mountains to the federal government, which led to the creation of the Southwest Territory. William Blount, who temporarily lived at Rocky Mount in Sullivan County, was named territorial governor.

Tennessee was later admitted to the Union on June 1, 1796, and Sevier, who previously led the state of Franklin, was elected governor.

The original Franklin capitol building was dismantled, placed on a barge, and transported to Nashville for the Tennessee Centennial Exposition in 1897. The cabin's logs apparently became lost, because a replica was eventually constructed in 1966 at the Greeneville site when the logs were not returned to the city, according to a historic marker.

BRIDGE BURNERS

Who burned bridges during the Civil War?

An open field in rural western Greene County is home to the final resting place of five Union soldiers who died during the Civil War and a monument reminding visitors of the infamous Bridge Burners.

The site is located along Pottertown Road at a family cemetery. It is surrounded by a mixture of farmland and industrial facilities. While visiting the site, guests will be likely to hear the sounds of nearby tractors cutting grass and semitrucks traveling down the road.

Desperate times call for desperate measures.

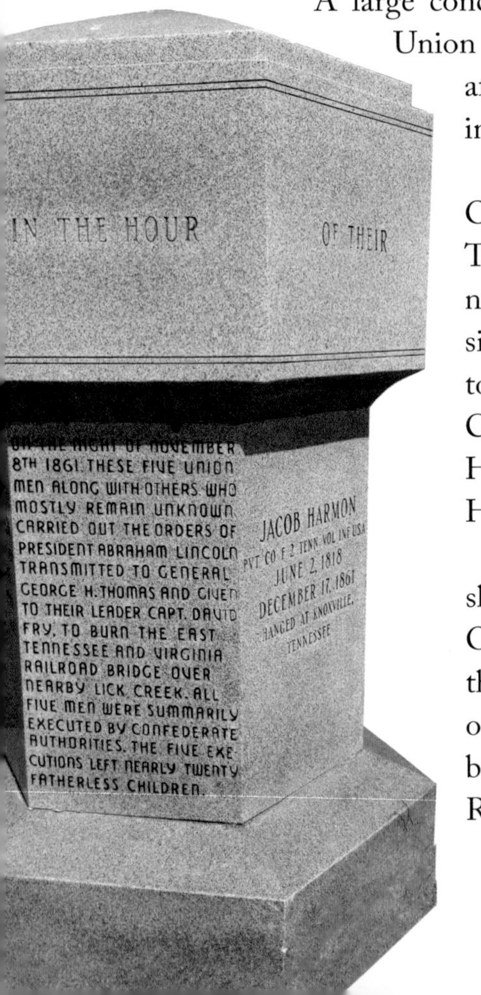

A large concrete monument memorializes five Union men who were executed in 1861 after being ordered to burn bridges in East Tennessee.

The phrase "IN THE HOUR OF THEIR COUNTRY'S PERIL, THEY WERE LOYAL" is embossed near the top of the memorial. Five sides of the monument are dedicated to the five men, identified as Christopher Haun, Henry Fry, Jacob Hinshaw, Jacob Harmon, and Henry Harmon.

The sixth side of the monument shares the story of the Bridge Burners. On the night of November 8, 1861, the five men carried out the orders of President Abraham Lincoln to burn the East Tennessee and Virginia Railroad Bridge over nearby Lick

The Bridge Burners memorial sits in the middle of farmland and industrial facilities in western Greene County, Tennessee.

Creek, the text on the monument states.

All five men were executed by Confederate authorities.

More details about the Bridge Burners can be found on a nearby kiosk. The historic Harmon family cemetery is also on-site.

Other bridge-burning efforts were reported in the Bluff City area as well as Strawberry Plains, Chattanooga, and Loudon in East Tennessee.

BRIDGE BURNERS MEMORIAL

WHAT: A solemn memorial in western Greene County, Tennessee, is dedicated to a handful of Civil War veterans.

WHERE: 1270 Pottertown Rd., Midway, TN 37809

COST: Free

PRO TIP: While in the Midway community, take a drive to the historic Bible Covered Bridge along Warrensburg Road near Bible Branch Road.

TO IMPEACH A PRESIDENT

Would you vote to impeach President Andrew Johnson?

In May of 1868, the United States Senate acquitted President Andrew Johnson of impeachment charges. The House of Representatives previously voted to impeach, but because the Senate did not approve the charges, Johnson, the 17th president, remained in office.

Every day, visitors to the Andrew Johnson National Historic Site in Greeneville can learn about the former president's life and cast their own vote.

Visitors are given a replica of the ticket used to gain entry to the impeachment trial. In the museum, guests have an opportunity to learn more about the circumstances regarding the charges, and they are encouraged to tear the end tab from their ticket and vote in a ballot box on Johnson's acquittal or guilt, according to the National Park Service.

On May 26 of each year, on the anniversary of the second Senate vote, employees tally the visitor results.

In 1868, the margin of acquittal was only one vote. Today, a majority of visitors often vote not guilty, according to the historic site.

The historic impeachment vote followed months of tensions between Johnson and Congress after the Civil War. The tensions came to a climax when Congress passed the Tenure of Office Act,

---

The Andrew Johnson National Historic Site features two homes, a tailor shop, a visitors center and museum, and the national cemetery, where the former president and his family are buried.

Andrew Johnson of Greeneville, Tennessee, served as the nation's 17th president. Photo courtesy of the Library of Congress.

which denied the president the authority to dismiss members of his cabinet without approval from Congress. Johnson vetoed the act, but Congress overrode his veto.

Later, Johnson dismissed Secretary of War Edwin Stanton, which led the House of Representatives to impeach the president.

IMPEACHMENT OF PRESIDENT ANDREW JOHNSON

WHAT: The public can decide whether to impeach a president at the Andrew Johnson National Historic Site in Greeneville.

WHERE: 101 N College St., Greeneville, TN 37743

COST: Free

PRO TIP: Be sure to visit each of the president's homes, as well as the national cemetery, which offers a spectacular view of the nearby mountains.

CANNONBALL HOUSE

Where can I find evidence of the Civil War in Blountville?

A fierce battle was fought in the town of Blountville on September 22, 1863. Federal forces advanced from Knoxville and arrived on the outskirts of Blountville. The forces quickly occupied the area overlooking the west side of Blountville. Soldiers aimed their cannons toward Confederate forces.

Southern forces reacted by forming artillery lines. The artillery and cavalry began battling, with the county courthouse becoming the first target.

The battle lasted several days. The Union dislodged the Confederates, who began to withdraw to nearby Bluff City. But the Confederate withdrawal was a preplanned, surprise counterattack, which ultimately led the Union forces to leave Blountville and head toward Knoxville.

Casualties were light, but the town of Blountville, one of the state's oldest communities, was devastated. The courthouse was gutted by fire, and businesses and homes were destroyed.

CANNONBALL HOUSE

WHAT: The Cannonball House was damaged during the Battle of Blountville.

WHERE: 3382 Tennessee State Route 126, Blountville, TN 37617

COST: Donations accepted

PRO TIP: The Civil War Trail in Tennessee includes several sites in Blountville, Bristol, Bluff City, and Elizabethton. For more information, visit civilwartrails.org.

A small portion of the Cannonball House's clapboard siding was slightly damaged on September 22, 1863, during the Battle of Blountville.

The Cannonball House in Sullivan County, Tennessee, was struck and damaged by Union cannon fire during the Battle of Blountville in 1863.

Only a few historic structures and homes survived the battle, including sites on the Civil War Trail such as the Blountville Cemetery, Sullivan County Courthouse, Old Deery Inn, and the Cannonball House.

The Cannonball House, also known as the Miller-Haynes House, is located on the main thoroughfare of the historic district. The home sustained structural damage from Union cannon fire.

According to a historical marker on the property, Elbert S. Miller bought the house in 1849 but sold it before the Civil War to Matthew T. Haynes and his wife, Kate Snapp Haynes. Haynes was a Confederate official whose job was to acquire property that had been commandeered from Unionists, the marker states.

The clapboard-sided house was caught in the middle of a Battle of Blountville skirmish, during which Union cannonballs hit the west side of the home, doing minor damage.

The Cannonball House is now owned by the nearby United Methodist Church. The only visible evidence of the Civil War is the little section on the left side of the home that is preserved with plexiglass, local historian Shelia Hunt said.

PORTABLE CHURCH

Why has a church in Blountville been moved three times to three separate counties?

A small log structure, originally built in the late 1700s, stands today in the serene Fellowship Park in Blountville.

That structure wasn't originally built across from the First Baptist Church of Blountville. Actually, throughout its long history, this portable building has been located in three separate locations in three separate counties in Northeast Tennessee.

The building, which has always served as a church, was first built in the late 1700s near Mountain City, Tennessee, although the exact spot is not known.

In the late 1950s, it was moved to Elizabethton along present-day West Elk Avenue, where Clyde "Fudd" Campbell collected local antiquities, including historic structures. Campbell's "Fuddtown" also featured the former Stover house, which was located outside of Elizabethton, and is where former President Andrew Johnson died.

The collection of historic buildings remained at the site until the early 21st century, when the assets at the site were auctioned off to the public.

A local physician purchased the Stover house and relocated it to the historic Brooks Farm in Carter County where it remains today. The log church structure was purchased and donated to the First Baptist Church in Blountville by JoAnn Steele in memory of her husband, John H. Steele.

It was relocated to Fellowship Park along Tennessee State Highway 126 after spending a year in storage. The log church features antique handmade pews and handmade furniture from the Steele family home, according to a marker at the park.

The log church at Blountville, Tennessee's, Friendship Park was originally built near Mountain City, Tennessee.

First Baptist dedicated the park in 2007. It includes the log church, a replica of the original First Baptist Church, a pavilion, a walking path, and other recreational facilities. The church replica is used for weddings, conferences, and other public events.

FELLOWSHIP PARK

WHAT: Fellowship Park in Blountville, Tennessee, is home to a church that has been located at one time or another in one of three communities.

WHERE: Along Tennessee State Route 126 in Blountville, TN 37617

COST: Free

PRO TIP: While here, be sure to visit other sites in the Blountville Historic District, including the historic Deery Inn and several buildings that have been relocated to the inn's grounds.

RUNWAY CEMETERY

Where is the hidden cemetery at Tri-Cities Airport?

At least 26 people were buried at Yoakley Cemetery in Blountville between 1844 and 1921. Those wanting to visit the historic cemetery, however, must be escorted by maintenance or security at Tri-Cities Airport.

The Yoakley Cemetery is one of the only cemeteries in the country to be located entirely within the security perimeter of a commercial airport. The few other similar graveyards can be found in Chicago, Illinois; Raleigh, North Carolina; and Savannah, Georgia.

"Periodically, by appointment only, staff will escort people to the cemetery for brief visits," said deputy director David Jones.

The cemetery was first established in 1844 on what was then farmland. Eliza Jane Yoakley, Rachel Paulina Yoakley, and Peter Lafayette Yoakley were the first three to be buried there. All three died at a young age, according to cemetery records.

The final person to be buried at Yoakley Cemetery, Sarah Ford, died in 1921. Remaining stones show that members of the Calton, Ford, Hakes, Hickam, Roller, and Yoakley families are all buried there.

More than a decade after Sarah Ford was buried, officials decided to establish an airport on the property. Jones said he believes the airport's planners did not move the Yoakley Cemetery because it does not affect operations and visitation to the cemetery is minimal.

While Yoakley Cemetery is within the confines of the airport security perimeter, guests can easily access Wheeler Cemetery, located entirely outside of the fence on the south side of the airport. More than 200 people are buried at Wheeler Cemetery, which can be reached via Hamilton Road.

The old gravestones of Yoakley Cemetery are located within the security perimeter of Tri-Cities Airport in Blountville, Tennessee.

CEMETERY AT THE AIRPORT

WHAT: A small cemetery is confined within the security perimeter at Tri-Cities Airport.

WHERE: 2525 Tennessee State Route 75, Blountville, TN 37617

COST: Free

PRO TIP: The cemetery can be seen from the highway, but visitors can also call ahead and ask to see the graves.

The Tri-Cities Regional Airport was originally opened in the 1930s as McKellar Field, in dedication of Senator Kenneth McKellar, an avid supporter of aviation in Tennessee.

The airport began as a collaborative effort between Johnson City, Bristol, Kingsport, and Sullivan County to build a regional airport that would serve the aviation needs of the area, as the smaller airfields in each city were no longer practical.

A Tri-City Airport Commission was formed to develop and operate the airport. The commission was made up of representatives from the participating municipalities. In 1935, plans were put into motion to construct the new airport.

While Yoakley Cemetery is the only graveyard within the security perimeter of the airport, a couple other cemeteries have also been noted in the immediate vicinity. Another graveyard, Deck Cemetery, no longer exists. The cemetery was located on present-day airport property, but graves were relocated for runway construction. They were moved to Wheeler Cemetery, Tri-Cities Memory Gardens, or to Blountville.

BACKYARD TERRORS

Is that a dinosaur?

Dinosaurs roam the woods of a property in Bluff City. There, the blockbuster film *Jurassic Park* comes alive. In 2007, Chris Kastner, the founder and owner of the Backyard Terrors Dinosaur Park, built his first life-size dinosaur.

Kastner said he had no idea what he was doing. He took a *Jurassic Park* magazine and tried to recreate one of the creatures in an image. He used scrap wood for the frame, wire for the muscles, and foam for the skin. Eventually, he discovered a vinyl material with which to coat the dinosaurs.

To perfect a dinosaurs' details, Kastner uses epoxy for the heads, hands, claws, and other intricate body parts.

After building the first dinosaur, people began stopping by the property to take pictures. A few gave donations, and a donation box was eventually installed.

BACKYARD TERRORS

WHAT: Backyard Terrors Dinosaur Park in Bluff City, Tennessee, features dozens of life-size dinosaur statues.

WHERE: 1065 Walnut Grove Rd., Bluff City, TN 37618

COST: Minimum $5 donation requested

PRO TIP: Visit the attraction on select evenings during the summer for a rather terrifying "Dinosaur Park in the Dark" event.

The owners of Backyard Terrors in Bluff City, Tennessee, have created numerous life-size dinosaurs for visitors to explore. Photos courtesy of Backyard Terrors.

Once Kastner received enough donations, he began building more dinosaurs. Pathways, landscaping, a gift shop, a picnic area, and a play area now accompany replicas of about 80 dinosaur species. More creatures are coming, Kastner said.

Backyard Terrors Dinosaur Park, which features a mix of nature, art, and science, covers several acres of land along Walnut Grove Road in Bluff City. Each sculpture includes the scientific name of the dinosaur along with info on the species. There's also an interactive section for children to learn by discovering hidden fossils.

The park is open from 9 a.m. to 9 p.m. daily. This is a donation-based attraction, and tours are self-guided. All donations and gift shop purchases will benefit the park's future expansion plans to keep providing a fun interactive experience to the public.

For more information about the park, call 423-391-7017 or email them at backyardterrors@gmail.com.

Months of research go into each addition at Backyard Terrors, resulting in lifelike prehistoric creatures wandering around the woods.

GO UNDERGROUND!

Where can I go spelunking in the Appalachian Highlands?

The Appalachian Highlands region, especially the Bluff City, Blountville, and Bristol areas, has long been known for its karst (porous limestone) geography. The "karstland," as it's called, is riddled with caves and sinkholes.

Two caves, Appalachian Caverns and Bristol Caverns, welcome thousands of visitors every year. Then, there is Worley's Cave in Bluff City, an off-the-grid sort of attraction that is not regularly open to the public.

The *Kingsport Times-News* featured the cave in an article back in 1965.

"Every summer, Worley's Cave in rural Bluff City gets more popular, and every summer, Mrs. Jim Boling's patience wears thinner," the newspaper reported. "But it's a fact as natural as the wonder itself: you can't keep boys out of dark, mysterious places any more than you can hold back the water that gouges out the rock."

Spelunkers, some as far away as Massachusetts, have wandered into the cave.

The cave has been mapped out to about 4.5 miles with many other side adventures along the way, according to the Watson family, which owns the property.

Historians say that the cave was used for mining saltpeter for ammunition during the Civil War. The original landowner was Elias S. Worley, the cave's namesake.

The natural attraction has also been called Morril's Cave due to John Morril's numerous explorations into the cave.

Worley's Cave does not feature lights or handrails for visitors. It's a living, wet, and natural cave.

Several area outfitters can take visitors through Worley's Cave, which features all types of natural cave features. Photos courtesy of USA Raft Adventure Resort.

WORLEY'S CAVE

WHAT: Worley's Cave is a popular spot for spelunking in Bluff City, Tennessee.

WHERE: 461 Timber Ridge Rd., Bluff City, TN 37618

COST: Price varies

PRO TIP: Don't go alone. Be sure to go on a guided spelunking tour of the cave.

A few area outfitters take guests on tours of the cave, including USA Raft Adventures.

Like other local caverns, the cave remains at about 55 degrees Fahrenheit, making it a great year-round adventure. Guests can explore the beauty of the natural cave features and formations and learn about the life and geology of an undeveloped, living limestone cave.

Worley's Cave requires no prior caving experience according to USA Raft.

For those concerned about tight spaces, there are none that require prolonged crawling, the organization states. The company provides gear and an experienced guide.

USA Raft guides will take you wherever you are comfortable, although Worley's Cave is not as developed for tourists as other local caverns.

ICON OF COUNTRY MUSIC

How did Lesley Riddle influence country music?

Lesley Riddle, an African American musician, may be one of the most influential figures in country music, but you may have never heard of him. Riddle, who grew up in Kingsport, was associated with the iconic Carter family, who have often been recognized as the founding family of country music.

Riddle, who is honored with a historic marker in downtown Kingsport, introduced A. P. Carter to songs of African American origin, which Carter reconfigured and brought into the family's repertoire. Riddle is considered one of the foundational blocks of American music, according to the Tennessee Music Pathways program.

In the 1920s and 1930, history shows that Black and White musicians came together in ways that simply made music better.

Riddle, who was born in Burnsville, North Carolina, in 1905, traveled with the Carters to collect songs throughout the region.

LESLEY RIDDLE

WHAT: Lesley Riddle was an influential musician who worked with the iconic Carter family during country music's early days.

WHERE: 400 Clinchfield St., Kingsport, TN 37660

COST: Free

PRO TIP: Visit tnvacation.com/tennessee-music-pathways to learn more about the Tennessee Music Pathways and discover the region's music history and heritage.

The Tennessee Music Pathways program recognizes several area musicians, including Lesley Riddle, Brownie McGhee, and Tennessee Ernie Ford.

A Tennessee Music Pathways marker recognizes African American musician Lesley Riddle in downtown Kingsport, Tennessee, along Broad Street.

He helped transcribe and adapt songs and hymns. He also helped shape Maybelle Carter's guitar techniques.

The Carter family recorded at the Bristol Sessions in 1927, which led Bristol to become known as the Birthplace of Country Music. The family went on to produce many songs and albums and became international stars in the 1920s.

"Sadly, Riddle never made his living in music himself; however, it is his contribution to country music for which he is most remembered," a Birthplace of Country Music blogger wrote.

Riddle had just one leg due to a cement factory accident. After the accident, Riddle took an interest in the guitar and mandolin.

After the onset of the Great Depression in 1929, record sales slumped dramatically, and by the early '30s, Carter could no longer afford to pay Riddle to accompany him, the historic marker states. Riddle then married and moved to Rochester, New York, where he worked as a clothes presser, shoeshine parlor operator, and school crossing guard, the marker states.

Before he died in 1979, Riddle did return to attend and perform at music festivals.

LONG ISLAND ICED TEA

What is the connection between Long Island iced tea and Tennessee?

Ask some folks in the Kingsport area about Long Island iced tea, and they'll quickly tell you, no, the popular alcoholic beverage is not from New York.

Many sources around the world often credit the drink's invention to Robert Butt, who is said to have created the cocktail in 1972 during a bartending contest when he was working at the Oak Beach Inn on Long Island, New York.

But Long Island iced tea was first produced about 50 years earlier on Long Island in Kingsport during the 1920s.

"We feel pretty certain that a lot of people in Kingsport and in the region aren't aware that the Long Island iced tea was born here (on Long Island)," Jud Teague, Executive Director of Visit Kingsport, said in a 2017 press release. "The drink has a long and very interesting history and we just felt like it was time for us to embrace it and our role in its creation."

Visit Kingsport claims the drink was first created during Prohibition when Charlie "Old Man" Bishop invented the concoction.

At the time, the four-mile-long island in the South Holston River was well known for its colorful characters and bootlegging activities. Bishop, known as an illegal liquor distiller, created a new drink by mixing rum, vodka, whiskey, gin, and tequila with a bit of maple syrup, the release stated.

About 20 years later, Bishop's son, Ransom, who operated a still on Long Island, tweaked his father's original recipe by adding lemon, lime, and cola.

Long Island, which was established in 1760, was an important site for each of the Cherokee, colonial pioneers, and early settlers of the region, respectively. It also served as a staging ground for

The Long Island Iced Tea *mural in downtown Kingsport, Tennessee, features the key ingredients in the original recipe, including maple syrup, lemon, and lime.*

westward travelers and a treaty site. Today, the island consists of a city park and Eastman Chemical Company.

A new mural in downtown Kingsport recognizes the city as the birthplace of Long Island iced tea. The artwork was painted on the backside of the Reserve cocktail bar on Center Street by local artist Helen Shivell.

LONG ISLAND ICED TEA

WHAT: Kingsport, Tennessee, claims to be the birthplace of Long Island iced tea.

WHERE: Behind 201 E Center St., Kingsport, TN 37660

COST: Free

PRO TIP: Check out the Kingsport Tea Trail, which includes more than a dozen businesses, to get a taste of local Long Island iced tea.

BIG JOHN

Why is there a giant Native American standing along Stone Drive in Kingsport?

The giant Native American statue standing in front of Pratt's BBQ has been an iconic landmark in Kingsport for more than a half century.

When John D. Barker returned to Kingsport after World War II, he had a few thousand dollars on hand with which to open a business. He opened Honest John's Trading Post, a store and curio shop.

Barker said the business struggled at first, but when he decided to construct a giant Native American statue out front, the money started rolling in.

A few years later, construction began on US Highway 11W, diverting traffic from Barker's original store and Native American statue on Chestnut Ridge. He decided to open up a new location on Highway 11W, so he moved the statue with the store.

The Pratt family later purchased the property in the early 1970s and has operated a restaurant ever since.

The giant Native American statue continues to attract visitors to the Pratt's Barn, where they serve delicious barbecue.

Current owner Tom Pratt has kept the statue because "he's good for business." The statue suffered a broken neck a few years ago and it was repaired. It's also been repainted and touched up over the years.

PRATT'S BBQ

WHAT: The *Big John* statue stands in front of the Pratt's BBQ restaurant in Kingsport.

WHERE: 1225 E Stone Dr., Kingsport, TN 37660

COST: Free, or enjoy a great barbecue meal at Pratt's.

PRO TIP: Visit on Sunday afternoon and enjoy the Pratt's lunch buffet.

Today, it's hard to miss the 39-foot-tall statue as one proceeds down Stone Drive through one of Kingsport's busiest commercial districts.

The Big John *statue, originally located on Chestnut Ridge in Kingsport, Tennessee, now stands in front of Pratt's BBQ on East Stone Drive.*

SANTA STATUE

Why is there a Santa statue in downtown Kingsport all year long?

Nearly every year since 1943, a train loaded with goodies for children has made its way across the Appalachian coalfields into downtown Kingsport. In 2017, in recognition of the Santa Train's annual trip, a statue was unveiled at Kingsport's Centennial Park.

The artwork, created by Bristol, Tennessee, artist Val Lyle is called *Spirit of Generosity*. It was inspired by the 75th anniversary of the Santa Train and the many acts of generosity that have made it possible.

The park, which celebrated the 100th anniversary of the city of Kingsport, is located next to the historic train depot on Main Street.

Every year, with a few exceptions, the Santa Train travels from Pikeville, Kentucky, to Kingsport on the Saturday before Thanksgiving in celebration of the holiday season. The Santa Train makes 14 stops in Kentucky, Virginia, and Tennessee, distributing more than 15

SANTA TRAIN

WHAT: A Santa Claus statue stands near the old railroad station in downtown Kingsport.

WHERE: 245 E Main St., Kingsport, TN 37660

COST: Free

PRO TIP: Centennial Park is great, but it comes alive when the Santa Train comes through in November.

Artist Val Lyle of Bristol has created many pieces of public artwork in the Appalachian Highlands region, including Kingsport's *Spirit of Generosity* and *Take the Stage* at Bristol's Cumberland Square Park.

Santa Claus keeps a watchful eye on the citizens of Kingsport, Tennessee, all year long while checking his Naughty or Nice List.

tons and $300,000 worth of clothing, food, candy, toys, and gifts to thousands of people.

In 1943, a delegation of Kingsport merchants, staff members from the Kingsport newspaper, and the Clinchfield Railroad Company traveled to Elkhorn City, Kentucky. The delegation met up with Santa Claus and traveled by rail back to Kingsport. For many years, treats were thrown from the train to children along the route. Eventually, the Santa Train crew dispersed toys, clothes, and other items.

In recent years, CSX, Food City, the Kingsport Chamber of Commerce, Appalachian Power, and Soles4Souls, have sponsored the event.

Centennial Park comes alive the Saturday before Thanksgiving each year with the Christmas spirit. It typically features live music, food, activities for the kids, and the arrival of the Santa Train as it makes its last stop in Kingsport.

GIVE EASTMAN A HAND

What does the giant hand symbolize at Eastman Chemical Company headquarters in Kingsport?

The Old Hand stands in front of Eastman Chemical Company's global headquarters in Kingsport. The stainless-steel sculpture depicts a hand manipulating a methanol molecule and represents the many hands that have guided the company and the many hands that will lead it through the next century, according to a media release from the company, which celebrated its centennial in 2020.

A small sculpture of an acetic acid molecule sits in front of Building 215 in recognition of the company's beginnings.

According to their website, *The Old Hand*, which is located in front of Eastman's headquarters on Wilcox Drive, was unveiled in the summer of 2021. It "stands 23 feet tall, 9 feet wide, 25 and a half inches long and extends 15 feet," the company write-up said. "The hand and arm sculpture consists of 300 plates welded together, while the methanol molecule consists of 192 individual plates." The article stated that the entire sculpture weighs more than 6,000 pounds.

The company said *The Old Hand* honors Eastman's beginnings distilling methanol from wood pulp. In addition, Eastman, which was incorporated in Kingsport in 1920 to provide raw materials for Eastman Kodak's photographic business, said methanolysis will play a significant role in the company's future as it builds one of the world's largest plastic-to-plastic molecular recycling facilities in Kingsport. Acetic acid, which continues to be critical to the production of several products manufactured at the Kingsport site, was selected as the molecule for the smaller part of the sculpture.

Over its first decade of operation, the Kingsport Eastman site expanded to include products like nonflammable X-ray

The Old Hand is a giant stainless-steel sculpture that sits in front of the global headquarters of Eastman Chemical Company in Kingsport.

film and charcoal briquettes. By 1994, the Eastman Chemical Company spun off from Eastman Kodak to become an independent corporation, which produces everything from innovative films for electric vehicles to recycled materials for sustainable water bottles and cosmetic cases.

THE OLD HAND

WHAT: Eastman Chemical Company unveiled *The Old Hand* in 2021 in Kingsport, Tennessee.

WHERE: 200 S Wilcox Dr., Kingsport, TN 37660

COST: Free

PRO TIP: Eastman Chemical Company's business center is not open to the public, but it is easy to see *The Old Hand* in front of the building.

FOOD IN A FLASH

Where should I go to have an outstanding burger and fries in the Appalachian Highlands?

It is really no secret to locals; Pal's Sudden Service is one of the best regional fast-food restaurant chains in the country.

With 31 locations in Tennessee and Virginia, Pal's is known for its quick-service American fare, such as the hot dog, Big Pal burger, Sauceburger, milkshakes, and Frenchie Fries. Oh yeah, and in the morning, be sure to order the cheddar rounds. You won't regret it. Patrons of Pal's can also order a Dr. Enuf, a soft drink based in Johnson City.

The first Pal's opened in 1956 in Kingsport a year after the restaurant's founder, Fred "Pal" Barger, attended a National Restaurant Convention in Chicago and met Ray Kroc and Fred Turner, observing the construction and equipment they used for the first McDonald's.

Pal's Sudden Service received the Malcolm Baldrige National Quality Award in 2001. It was the first restaurant to receive the award.

Pal's is often studied and reviewed by the competition due to its unique training culture, which includes pop quizzes and more than 200 hours of instruction.

PAL'S SUDDEN SERVICE

WHAT: Pal's Sudden Service has been named one of the best local fast-food chains in the country and is known for its unique architecture.

WHERE: As of 2023, Pal's Sudden Service had 31 locations in Tennessee and Virginia. Its original location is at 327 Revere St., Kingsport, TN 37660.

COST: Everything under $6 each

PRO TIP: Go in the morning and try the cheddar rounds. Unfortunately, they're not available after breakfast.

Want to find a Pal's in a flash? It's not too difficult. Be on the lookout for its unique novelty architecture, featuring large replicas of food items placed on the roof. The giant burger, hot dog, fries, and drink can be found at most locations. A giant man holds a burger on the roof of the Pal's on Lynn Garden Drive while the original location near downtown features a red-and-white motif.

It's no wonder Pal's is often ranked among the best regional chains in the country. Just check out lists from *Food & Wine* and *USA Today*.

Artists Karen and Tony Barone of Southern California originally fabricated the unique giant food replicas found on the roofs of Pal's restaurants around the region.

Most Pal's locations feature a giant replica burger, hot dog, drink, and fries. Photo courtesy of the Library of Congress.

STONE CASTLE

How many high schools get to play football in a castle?

Maybe just one. High school students at Tennessee High School in Bristol play football every Friday night during the fall at the Stone Castle, a beloved medieval-style structure in the middle of the city.

The Stone Castle features arched entries, 20-foot-high crenelated walls, and unusual corner towers. The walls of the fortresslike stadium can be viewed from Weaver Pike, Edgemont Avenue, and Southside Avenue.

Construction began in 1934, and the cost was shared between Bristol and the federal government. The Works Progress Administration, a federal Great Depression–era agency, completed the Stone Castle. Crews pulled limestone from a nearby construction project along Beaver Creek in Sullivan County to build the fortress. The first football game occurred there in 1936. It is one of two WPA stadiums still in use in Tennessee; the other is across the state in Memphis.

The Stone Castle is not just a venue for football. Over the years, the Stone Castle has been used for various activities, including track and field events, graduation ceremonies, and band competitions. The Southeastern Band Festival and the Music in the Castle competitions have attracted thousands of high school band members and their families to the Stone Castle since 1951.

"Music in the Castle is a unique experience for students to play in a unique venue that makes them feel like they have gone

---

The Stone Castle is listed on the National Register of Historic Places as Bristol Memorial Stadium. It was added to the register in 1987 for its unique architecture.

The Stone Castle in Bristol, Tennessee, was constructed of limestone from nearby Beaver Creek.

back in time," said Tennessee High School Director of Bands David Semones. "Everyone is able to experience wonderful bands inside the castle."

The Stone Castle has been used in the past as a home football field for Virginia, Slater, and Douglass High Schools. Local colleges have also used the football stadium.

THE STONE CASTLE

WHAT: The Stone Castle is a unique stadium at Tennessee High School in Bristol.

WHERE: 1100 Edgemont Ave., Bristol, TN 37620

COST: Free to see, except during events

PRO TIP: The Stone Castle is great from the outside, but be sure to watch a Bristol Tennessee High School football game for the best experience.

HIDDEN STREET

Where is Bank Street in Bristol, and why should you go there?

Drive down State Street in Bristol and you might just pass up one of the city's most obscure thoroughfares. Narrow Bank Street stretches for about 400 feet between State Street and Shelby Street on the Tennessee side of the state line.

From State Street, it's hard to tell that Bank Street exists, but Jon Luttrell, director for community relations for the city of Bristol, Tennessee, confirms that Bank Street is an official city street. The northern half of the street closest to State Street, however, is closed to vehicle traffic and is for pedestrians only. The southern half is open to vehicular traffic and gives drivers access to the Bank Street parking lot.

"It was generally a path or alley in the early days to Shelby Street," said local historian Tim Buchanan. "There were a number of small businesses along Bank Street including a building that was used for the 1928 Bristol Sessions."

Most of the historic buildings are gone, but Buchanan said he remembers being able to drive the entire road between State and Shelby Streets. It was also important for access to the stage entrance to the historic Paramount theater. The street was named after a bank building located there that faced State Street.

In recent years, a painter created a large mural along Bank Street depicting various aspects and landmarks of Bristol. Twelve Bristol gems are featured on the mural, including the Bristol train station; the weir dam at South Holston Lake; Stone Castle at Tennessee

---

Downtown Bristol is home to several famous murals, such as the legendary country music mural, hand-painted by artist Tim White in 1986.

Several murals depicting local Bristol culture and history line the walls of Bank Street in downtown.

High School; Bristol Caverns; Steele Creek Park; Mendota Trail in Bristol, Virginia; Bristol Sign, State Street marker; Ron Necciai, a legendary Bristol baseball player; *The Wizard of Oz*, a beloved musical performed at the Paramount; and the Paramount organ. The artist used an actual photo of the front of Merchants Exchange Bank, which stood nearby, to create the bank teller for the mural.

Explore Bristol, Believe in Bristol, and members of the community developed the mural.

BANK STREET

WHAT: A beautiful and informative mural lines the walls of narrow Bank Street in Bristol, Tennessee.

WHERE: Bank St., Bristol, TN 37620

COST: Free

PRO TIP: Head on over to the Birthplace of Country Music Museum at 101 Country Music Way in Bristol, Virginia, to learn more about the region's music. Want to take a selfie? Go to Cumberland Square Park and check out the statues.

BRIDGE DEFENDER

What Bristolian is buried in two separate cemeteries?

His hand is buried in Strawberry Plains, but those looking for the grave memorial of Confederate Pvt. James Keeling can find the rest of him buried at Bristol's historic East Hill Cemetery.

Keeling stood guard at the Strawberry Plains railroad bridge in Jefferson County the night of November 8, 1861, when a dozen Unionists tried to burn it, according to the *Knoxville News-Sentinel*. The other guard ran. Keeling, also known as James Keelan, stayed and held off the attackers.

He suffered repeated gunshot and knife wounds, including an injury that cost him most of his left hand.

Bristol historian Bud Phillips said the attackers thought they had killed Keeling and rode away. Keeling walked nearly a quarter mile to the home of William Elmore who sent for Dr. Robert Sneed. The doctor amputated Keeling's injured hand, Phillips reported.

According to her diary, Sarah Stringfield, a granddaughter of Sarah King Williams, made a silk bag for the severed hand and early the next morning, it was buried in the family cemetery at the feet of her father, Rev. Thomas Stringfield, Phillips confirmed in an article in the *Bristol Herald Courier*.

Keeling survived the attack. Phillips said word spread of his heroic deed, and soon he was regarded as one of the Southern Confederate heroes. He ultimately earned recognition as "the

CONFEDERATE PRIVATE JAMES KEELING

WHAT: Confederate Pvt. James Keeling is buried at East Hill Cemetery in Bristol.

WHERE: Along State Street in Bristol

COST: Free

PRO TIP: East Hill Cemetery began with the burial of five-year-old Nellie Gaines in 1857.

James Keeling's grave site sits among dozens of unique concrete markers, obelisks, and stones at East Hill Cemetery in Bristol.

Horatius of the Confederacy," named after the legendary Roman sentry who defended a bridge across the Tiber River from invaders.

Keeling moved to Bristol and died in 1895 and was buried at the East Hill Cemetery, which straddles the Tennessee and Virginia line.

Located just outside a circle in the cemetery where most of the Confederate soldiers are buried, Keeling has a small, plain obelisk resting on a heavy base. "Defender of the Bridge" and a Confederate flag are near the apex of the obelisk, according to the National Register of Historic Places, which listed East Hill Cemetery in 2011.

Those looking for obscure finds will discover many at East Hill Cemetery, including the grave site of the Confederate Unknown, and the final resting place of Silas Goodson, a slave who was reportedly 130 years old when he died.

CATERPILLAR CRAWL

Have caterpillars inundated downtown Bristol?

Walk around downtown Bristol and you might find 10 bronze caterpillars captured in various stages of life—from birth to butterfly. The Caterpillar Crawl, first established along the state line between Tennessee and Virginia in 2009, takes families and children throughout downtown, showcasing the community's attractions.

It is a fun way to discover Bristol and to involve children. Pick up a brochure at the city library or chamber of commerce, follow the clues and map, and learn about the many unique features of downtown. The Junior League of Bristol created the scavenger hunt and based it off the book *The Very Hungry Caterpillar* by Eric Carle.

The project was designed to promote children's literacy with hands-on adventures based on the popular children's book, as well as a way for families to learn about Bristol. The initiative is fashioned after a similar project in Greenville, South Carolina, featuring mice.

The bronze caterpillars, created by local artist Val Lyle, start showing up at the farmers market and end at the city library.

As the brochure states, families will first head to the farmers market. Stop One can be found near the farmers market mural, the brochure states. Then, families will head toward Carter Family Way, which is named after the famed country music family. Here, the

Downtown Bristol can get busy. Be alert and watch for cars and other activity while walking through town.

This piece of caterpillar artwork can be found along State Street in downtown Bristol, not far from the famous Country Music Mural.

CATERPILLAR CRAWL

WHAT: The Caterpillar Crawl is a scavenger hunt in Bristol.

WHERE: Throughout downtown Bristol

COST: Free

PRO TIP: Take advantage of the route. There are several great eateries along the way, including Blackbird Bakery and Eatz on Moore Street.

caterpillar is "eating an apple today." It adds, "At the bank is where he'll be found, behind a column, on the ground."

The scavenger hunt takes families to various other spots, including a performance arts venue, a bakery, a restaurant, and a museum. By the end of the scavenger hunt, the caterpillar transitions into a cocoon and, finally, to a butterfly.

TENNESSEE–VIRGINIA LINE

Where can I stand in two states at one time?

Not many cities can claim to be divided by a state line. But that's the case between Bristol, Tennessee, and Bristol, Virginia.

Many people have stood on the state line, while dodging cars, to take a selfie. Dozens of brass markers rest in the pavement along the border on State Street, making them popular spots for selfies and family photos.

In 2016, the Geico Gecko came to Bristol, planted its feet on State Street, and made the city's decades-old brass markers known to the masses. The insurance company commercial asks viewers: Tenniginia or Virginessee?

Many stores, like Cranberry Lane on the Virginia side, sell custom souvenirs with the iconic street marker in the tagline.

Local historian Tim Buchanan said there has been a lot of misinformation shared about the markers over the years.

The markers were placed in State Street after it was resurfaced in September 1938, Buchanan said. The Downtown Merchants

STATE LINE

WHAT: There are many spots along the miles-long state line between Tennessee and Virginia where visitors can take a selfie to prove they're standing in two states at once.

WHERE: State Street in Bristol

COST: Free

PRO TIP: Need a state-line souvenir? Check out Cranberry Lane at 623 State St. in Bristol, Virginia.

The state line in Bristol can cause some confusion, such as what's legal and what's not? It often depends on the state.

The markers on State Street in downtown Bristol provide a perfect backdrop for photographs. Photo courtesy of Bristol Herald Courier.

Association recommended that both cities recognize the state line with markers, which were installed in May 1939. Buchanan said that, unfortunately, the organization's records have not been located regarding the markers.

In the fall of 1950, the markers were removed when State Street was resurfaced again. They were reinstalled in May 1951. Buchanan said, "It is a strong possibility that in 1951 they simply put the old ones back in the street and in the early 1960s new ones were put in."

After State Street was redesigned and resurfaced in 1983–1984, the ones currently in State Street were installed.

The historic Bristol sign, another state line landmark, has been welcoming visitors to State Street since the early 20th century. The Bristol Gas and Electric Company erected the sign atop a hardware store in 1910 to advertise the city.

The sign originally contained the lighted slogan "PUSH! – THAT'S BRISTOL." In 1915, the sign was moved to its current location. Then, in 1921, the sign changed to "A GOOD PLACE TO LIVE."

COUSIN ERNIE

What's so special about the unassuming house on Anderson Street?

The small frame home at 1223 Anderson Street in Bristol, Tennessee, is quite unassuming. Except for a small wood sign out front and a nearby state historic marker, no one would know who once lived in the house.

Built in the early 1900s, legendary musician and actor Tennessee Ernie Ford was born at the home in 1919.

Ford's early successes as a radio personality led to his signing with Capitol Records in 1949, according to the Bristol Chamber of Commerce. Through 1976, he released a total of 83 albums on the label, and many single records, including the classic "Sixteen Tons," which became a number one hit around the world.

In addition, Ford went on to be featured in several television shows, including iconic appearances on *I Love Lucy*, on which he portrayed Cousin Ernie.

His 1990 induction into the Country Music Hall of Fame; placement of three stars on the Hollywood Walk of Fame for his achievements in radio, television, and recordings; and receipt of the Presidential Medal of Freedom all reflect his status as one of America's top entertainers, according to the historic marker near the home.

In 1990, the Bristol Historical Association was in need of a meeting place and decided to purchase Ford's homeplace, with

---

Tennessee Ernie Ford, one of Bristol's most famous residents, recorded numerous albums and won countless awards and honors, including three stars on the Hollywood Walk of Fame and the Presidential Medal of Freedom.

Tennessee Ernie Ford, a legendary musician and actor, lived in an unassuming home on Anderson Street in Bristol, Tennessee.

TENNESSEE ERNIE FORD BIRTHPLACE

WHAT: Tennessee Ernie Ford lived in a home on Anderson Street in Bristol, Tennessee.

WHERE: 1223 Anderson St., Bristol, TN 37620

COST: Donation requested

PRO TIP: Planning a country music getaway? Visit Bristol's Birthplace of Country Music Museum, the Earnest Tube, and the historic markers along State Street near Martin Luther King Jr. Blvd.

his blessing. Ford, who died in 1991, attended the grand opening ceremony.

The restored home features a variety of memorabilia, plus furniture and other household items from the early 1900s. Many original features of the house also remain, such as a vintage cast-iron bathtub.

One room serves as a museum and contains many pieces of Ford memorabilia, as well as local country music history.

To arrange individual or group tours, contact the Bristol Historical Association at bristoltnva@aol.com or call 276-466-9116.

IT'S BRISTOL, BABY!

Where is the world's fastest half mile?

Since its first race in 1961, Bristol Motor Speedway has been one of the most popular and successful tracks on the NASCAR circuit.

Driver Dale Earnhardt Jr. grew up around the speedway watching the conquests of his iconic father Dale Sr. and coined a famous phrase after a sweep of victories during the 2004 Night Race.

After winning the Xfinity Series race the night before, Earnhardt Jr. became the first to double-up in a single weekend at Bristol.

Earnhardt Jr. climbed out of his red No. 8 Chevy in Victory Lane, and when NBC reporter Bill Weber asked the driver why the win was so special, he let out a roar that sent waves across the region, according to the speedway's recorded description of the iconic moment:

"It's Bristol, Baby!" Earnhardt said.

Those three short words live on today.

The phrase is plastered on mugs, shirts, banners, billboards, and across social media platforms each spring and fall when NASCAR fans converge on Bristol.

More than a decade later, Bristol Motor Speedway honored that iconic moment with a large "It's Bristol, Baby!" sign at the north entrance where visitors can take interactive pictures and selfies.

The speedway, which is far from a local secret, has garnered numerous records over the years. It's the world's largest amphitheater with a maximum capacity of 165,000, and the fourth-largest sports venue in the United States, behind non-amphitheaters like the Indianapolis Motor Speedway.

Since 1993, Bristol Motor Speedway has had a concrete track, but beginning in 2021, a dirt race has been held each spring.

Visitors can check out the "It's Bristol, Baby!" sign year-round at Bristol Motor Speedway. Inset photo courtesy of the National Archives.

IT'S BRISTOL, BABY!

WHAT: Bristol Motor Speedway has been called the "World's Fastest Half Mile" and the "Last Great Colosseum."

WHERE: 151 Speedway Blvd., Bristol, TN 37620

COST: Free, except for events

PRO TIP: Visit Bristol Motor Speedway during the holiday season when the property is decked out in thousands of Christmas lights.

In 2009, a Bristol crowd set a Guinness World Record for the largest karaoke performance when 160,000 people simultaneously sang "Friends in Low Places" by Garth Brooks. In 2016, Bristol broke the record for the largest attendance at an American football game when 130,045 people watched the University of Tennessee Volunteers beat the Virginia Tech Hokies.

Other records over the years have included the world's largest card section when 128,000 cards spelled out "USA" in 2007, as well as the world's largest crowd wave.

MIGHTY WURLITZER

What rare instrument can be found at the Paramount in Bristol?

A hidden treasure sits inside the historic Paramount Center for the Arts in Bristol, Tennessee. The theater is home to the Mighty Wurlitzer, a unique theater pipe organ that can only be found in a handful of theaters around the world.

Only two organs have ever graced the Paramount stage since it opened in February 1931. The original organ was dismantled in the 1950s, when the theater was remodeled. Later, when the theater was being restored in the late 1980s for its grand reopening, project leader Mary Beth Rainero and the Paramount's house organist Rex Ward began looking for a new theater organ. The pair received word from the Piedmont Theatre Organ Society that a Mighty Wurlitzer dating from about 1926 had suddenly become available.

This was quite remarkable as only a few dozen Mighty Wurlitzers, which are no longer

THE MIGHTY WURLITZER

WHAT: The Mighty Wurlitzer is a grand organ that still works at the historic Paramount Center for the Arts in Bristol, Tennessee.

WHERE: 518 State St., Bristol, TN 37620

COST: Free, except for events

PRO TIP: Call the Paramount at 423-274-8920 for a tour of the historic theater.

At the Paramount's reopening gala in 1991, the first thing the audience heard was "The Star-Spangled Banner" played on the Mighty Wurlitzer, which was also the first song played at the venue's original opening night.

The Mighty Wurlitzer at the Paramount in Bristol, Tennessee, is just one of a few dozen still used for performances. Photos courtesy of the Paramount.

built, remain. In the early 20th century, thousands of these gigantic pipe organs were installed in movie theaters throughout the US, Canada, England, and Australia to accompany silent movies, according to an article on the *Smithsonian* magazine's website.

The organ is valued at more than $700,000, but the Piedmont Theatre Organ Society leases it to Paramount Bristol for the sum of $1 per year.

"Miss Marlene," as the organ is affectionately named, was originally in the Paramount Theatre in Charlottesville, Virginia. They had one week to dismantle the organ and move it to Bristol.

Trucks and trailers were leased, and eager volunteers guided all the pieces to Bristol. The unique instrument, described as the only instrument that can reproduce the sound of a complete orchestra, all by one person, is stored under the orchestra pit and can be raised and lowered as needed by a hydraulic lift at stage left.

FORTY AND EIGHT

What's the story behind the old boxcar at the Bristol American Legion post?

One of Bristol's most important historical attractions may also be one of the least known. A railcar from the Merci Train sits outside of the American Legion chapter on Marion Avenue.

The Merci Train was a train of 49 French railroad boxcars filled with tens of thousands of gifts of gratitude from at least that many individual French citizens. The French were showing their appreciation for the more than 700 railroad boxcars of relief goods sent to them by Americans in 1948.

The Merci Train arrived in New York Harbor in the late 1940s. Each of the 48 states at the time received one of the boxcars. The 49th boxcar was shared by Washington, DC, and Hawaii, which was still a territory at the time. Parades and ceremonies were held throughout the country.

The Tennessee car arrived in Bristol in February of 1949 and was presented to the city on Front Street, which is now Martin Luther King Jr. Boulevard. The presentation followed a parade up State Street according to the *Bristol Herald Courier*.

Bristol's train contained books, pictures, and 1,600 packages of French cigarette papers as well as letters, which were distributed to Sullins and Virginia Intermont College, where students translated the messages. The cigarette papers were distributed to local veterans and community leaders.

Today, the Merci Train boxcar is parked under a canopy adjacent to the American Legion post.

The Merci Train boxcar often joins local veterans over the holidays for parades on State Street in Bristol.

One of 49 French railroad boxcars gifted to the United States in 1949 is located at the American Legion in Bristol, Tennessee.

MERCI TRAIN OF BRISTOL

WHAT: The Merci Train was a gift from France, and other such cars can be found across the country, including in Bristol, Tennessee.

WHERE: 515 Marion Ave., Bristol, TN 37620

COST: Free

PRO TIP: Planning a trip to learn about local veterans? Also check out the memorial at Cumberland Square Park in Bristol, Virginia, which features two Vietnam-era aircraft: a UH-1H Huey and an AH-1H Cobra.

An American Legion group known as the La Societe Des Quarante Hommes Et Huit Chevaux are the caretakers of the remaining cars. The group is known as the Forty and Eight, because the boxcars would hold 40 men and eight horses (also the translation of the group name).

During the war, soldiers often went to or from the battlefields in the same type of boxcar. There were no seats, no windows, no toilets, and no sleeping or dining accommodations. When the soldiers came back to America, they decided to make little gift boxcar memorials for their lost military companions. Today, those soldiers continue to care for the remaining boxcars. At least 43 of the 49 original Merci boxcars still exist, according to the organization.

HANK'S LAST STOP

Where was legendary country musician Hank Williams Sr. last seen alive?

Decades later, mystery still surrounds the death of Hank Williams Sr., who was en route from Alabama to Ohio.

One notable tale takes Williams, a legendary country music artist, to Bristol, Virginia, and the popular Burger Bar, located at the corner of State Street and Piedmont Avenue.

Between December 31, 1952, and New Year's Day, 1953, a 17-year-old college freshman named Charles Carr, on Christmas break from Auburn, drove Williams to a show in Canton, Ohio.

They stopped in Knoxville and stayed at the Andrew Johnson Hotel. Later, the pair drove the backroads through the Appalachian Mountains.

Williams and Carr are believed to have stopped in Bristol, where rumors say they visited the Burger Bar. Even Carr, who is still alive, isn't quite sure where they stopped, according to a recent article in the *Atlanta Journal-Constitution*.

Nonetheless, Williams, 29, was no longer living when they arrived at a hospital in Oak Hill, West Virginia, on New Year's Day. The official cause of death was listed as heart failure.

The Burger Bar has been a Bristol attraction since 1942 and serves the freshest, juiciest burgers available anywhere. The Deel family now owns the popular downtown eatery, continuing its long tradition.

BURGER BAR

WHAT: Country music legend Hank Williams Sr. is said to have visited the Burger Bar before he died.

WHERE: 120 Piedmont Ave., Bristol, VA 24201

COST: Prices vary on items.

PRO TIP: Not hungry? You can buy a souvenir Burger Bar T-shirt instead of lunch.

Celebrities and politicians often stop at the Burger Bar in Bristol, Virginia, including Governor Glenn Youngkin, pictured in top photo, and country music legend Hank Williams Sr., pictured in inset. Top photo courtesy of the Virginia Office of Governor. Inset photo courtesy of the Library of Congress.

Visitors will discover heaping helpings of nostalgia, such as vintage 45 rpm records that sit next to an album by Bristol native Tennessee Ernie Ford. Historic photos of Bristol hang on the walls.

The interior remains retro with checkerboard floors and a lunch counter, much like it was when Williams may have visited.

All of the burgers on the Burger Bar menu are named after Hank Williams Sr.'s songs, such as the "Cold, Cold Heart" and "Hey, Good Lookin'."

SOLAR HILL

How did the Solar Hill neighborhood get its unique name?

The Solar Hill neighborhood, which is marked with a monument along Cumberland Street, is located just north of the state line in Bristol, Virginia. This beautiful neighborhood, filled with historic homes and brick streets, overlooks downtown.

But how did Solar Hill get its heavenly name?

In 1869, astronomers from the nation's capital came to Bristol to view the solar eclipse. The town sat in the path of totality, the area where the sun is completely blocked by the passing of the moon. The sun was expected to be about 96 percent eclipsed in Bristol.

Astronomers were dispatched to observation points across the country, including Hannibal, Missouri; Oakland Station, Kentucky; and Bristol, Virginia, which was called Goodson at the time. The group that visited Bristol chose to construct an observatory on Solar Hill, which was then called Lancaster's Hill.

After the eclipse, the neighborhood became known as Solar Hill.

The *Bristol Herald Courier* reported that the astronomers had also sought to observe a planet between Mercury and the sun. That didn't happen.

With the exception of the King mansion, the acreage on Solar Hill in 1869 was primarily pasture and woodland. The Solar Hill property was purchased in 1871, and lots were soon subdivided and sold.

The neighborhood grew around the antebellum estate of James King Jr. It was incorporated into the city of Bristol in 1890,

---

The approximately 27-acre Solar Hill Historic District was added to the National Register of Historic Places in 2001.

With grand homes and monuments, Solar Hill is one of Bristol, Virginia's, most historic neighborhoods. Photo courtesy of Bristol Herald Courier.

which led to further development and the construction of a majority of its residences. Construction continued into the 1920s and 1930s.

SOLAR HILL

WHAT: The historic Solar Hill neighborhood is located on a rise between Piedmont and Commonwealth Avenues in Bristol, Virginia.

WHERE: Solar Hill Historic District, Bristol, VA 24201

COST: Free

PRO TIP: Visit and tour historic Emmanuel Episcopal Church in Solar Hill. The Gothic-style church was modeled after the 13th-century Church of St. James the Less in Sulgrave, England.

THE OFFSET AND TRIPOINT

Why is the border between Tennessee and Virginia not completely straight?

Take a look at a map of Tennessee and you'll notice the northeastern part of the state cuts for a few miles into its Virginia neighbor. This unusual boundary line is home to a community known as the Offset.

This odd corner in the state line between Tennessee and Virginia is part of an error in the boundary line that extends part of Tennessee into Virginia. A marker on the nearby Virginia Creeper Trail, just north of the Offset, features details on the unusual boundary line.

In 1749, the original surveying line, which is not far from Whitetop Gap Road, was begun far east of the marker by Peter Jefferson, the father of Thomas Jefferson.

At the time, Tennessee hadn't yet been created. Tennessee became a state in 1796.

Before Jefferson and fellow surveyor Joshua Fry drew the line, King Charles I in England gave all the land between the 31st and 36th parallel to Sir Robert Heath and named it Carolana. The 36th parallel line eventually became the northern border of North Carolina.

THE OFFSET

WHAT: The Offset is an obscure community along the Tennessee and Virginia border.

WHERE: Tennessee and Virginia state line, east of Bristol

COST: Free

PRO TIP: Plan a trip to the Offset while also visiting Green Cove Depot.

The TriPoint marks the spot where the states of North Carolina, Tennessee, and Virginia meet. Photos courtesy of Stanford Dailey.

In 1749, Jefferson and Fry developed a line to the Whitetop area and eastward. At the time, the area of Whitetop was sparsely populated and the line was discontinued.

In 1779, the boundary line was continued, but a discrepancy occurred, and a correction was made to bring the boundary back to its former place.

The land in the area of the discrepancy was called the Offset. Today, the Cherokee National Forest covers much of the Offset, along with some farmland and recreational areas.

The points created by the Offset have become historic landmarks such as the Tennessee point and the point where North Carolina, Virginia, and Tennessee meet at the TriPoint marker. Hikers can visit those points by forest service trails.

OLD MAUDE

Who was Old Maude and how was she captured at Green Cove?

O. Winston Link was one of the nation's most revered railroad photographers, and one of his most famous is of Old Maude trekking into the old Green Cove station in Virginia.

Link is known for capturing the end of the golden age of the railroad industry. His work on the Virginia Creeper railroad line symbolizes technology transforming the face of rural America.

The photo was not planned when Link visited the Green Cove station, which still stands today along the transformed Virginia Creeper Trail. He asked brothers Gene and Roy Hampton, who were driving the sledge pulled by their horse, Old Maude, and hauling wood to the family's nearby farm, to wait a few minutes for the train to pull into the station. What resulted was Link's famous photograph, which is memorialized today by a marker at Green Cove.

The Virginia Creeper once ran from Abingdon, Virginia, to Todd, North Carolina. It also passed through the communities of Damascus, Taylors Valley, Green Cove, and Whitetop.

A station was built at Green Cove in 1914 by the Virginia Carolina Railroad. It has served as not only a railroad station, but a post office, store, and community gathering spot. The last train passed through in 1977, but it stayed open for a few more years.

The Green Cove station is located on the Virginia Creeper Trail.

The Old Maude photograph is recognized on a marker outside of the Green Cove station.

Then, in the 1990s, the US Forest Service purchased the Green Cove station in order to restore and preserve the structure. Today, it serves as a rest stop, visitors center, and education center for visitors on the Virginia Creeper Trail.

Out front, visitors will also discover a stone marker celebrating the Old Maude photograph.

GREEN COVE STATION

WHAT: Old Maude was a horse that used to pull a sledge near the Virginia Carolina Railroad and she was beautifully captured in a photograph by O. Winston Link.

WHERE: 41259 Green Cove Rd., Damascus, VA 24236

COST: Free

PRO TIP: There are several bicycle shops in Abingdon and Damascus where visitors can rent a bike to travel the Virginia Creeper Trail.

Starting at Whitetop Station, the Virginia Creeper Trail meanders downhill and over some of the most beautiful scenery in the region, which includes farmland, forests, Christmas tree farms, streams, and restored depots.

THE RESTING TREE

What's the Resting Tree?

The Resting Tree is a remarkable natural and spiritual wonder located in Sugar Hollow Park in Bristol, Virginia. Enslaved African Americans who lived and worked on the Walnut Grove plantation gathered at the tree to rest and eventually were buried there.

Very limited documentation exists regarding the slave cemetery, especially since most of the crudely made markers have long since disappeared, according to the Bristol Historical Association.

The tree, an oak, remains in excellent condition. It measures 15.6 feet in circumference and 57 inches in diameter, according to Remarkable Trees, a Virginia Tech Department of Forest Resources and Environmental Conservation project. It is 85 feet in height and has been allowed to grow in its natural state for centuries.

The Resting Tree Cemetery, which is now documented by a historical marker, was once part of the 920-acre Walnut Grove plantation owned by Colonel Robert Preston. Only three uninscribed fieldstone grave markers remain intact.

The Virginia Tech report claims that, according to local tradition, the Preston slaves sought the shade of this large oak tree to meet with their children during their daily work breaks. The burial near the tree of a child named Dan in 1798 and of an elderly person named Reuben in 1803 led to the establishment of this place as a cemetery, the report states.

Sugar Hollow Park is a 400-acre city-owned park in Bristol, Virginia, and features athletic fields, picnic sites, a campground, a playground, and trails.

The massive 85-foot-high Resting Tree is located at Sugar Hollow Park in Bristol, Virginia.

It goes on to explain that the cemetery remained in use during the 19th century and continued as a spiritual place for the African American community, even after the abolishment of slavery. Although today the cemetery is largely neglected, the giant oak remains as a witness to testify for a now silent community who once looked to it for strength.

RESTING TREE

WHAT: The Resting Tree is a historic site at Sugar Hollow Park in Bristol, Virginia.

WHERE: 21371 Forsythe Rd., Bristol, VA 24202

COST: Free

PRO TIP: Sugar Hollow Park is a great place to enjoy nature, including the Resting Tree, wetlands, and a cave.

ALL THE WORLD'S A CHURCH

Did you know the state theater of Virginia used to be a church?

Barter Theatre first opened its doors on June 10, 1933, during the Great Depression. The venue proclaimed: "With vegetables you cannot sell, you can buy a good laugh." The price of admission was 40 cents or an equivalent amount of produce. Four out of five visitors paid their way with vegetables, dairy products, and livestock, according to Barter Theatre.

The beautiful theater, located along historic Main Street in downtown Abingdon, is housed in a former church—one of the community's longest-serving congregations.

Sinking Spring Presbyterian Church, which now stands just up the street from the present-day Barter Theatre, was first established in the early 1700s. Sinking Creek's first church facility, a log structure, was originally located at the present-day Sinking Spring Cemetery. A larger building was later constructed in the 1780s, according to a written history about the church.

In 1831, a third structure was built on Main Street—the building that now houses Barter. The building was later sold in 1890 to the Sons of Temperance and was called Temperance Hall for many years.

BARTER THEATRE

WHAT: Barter Theatre is the official state theater of Virginia and is located in historic downtown Abingdon.

WHERE: 127 W Main St., Abingdon, VA 24210

COST: Prices vary.

PRO TIP: Check out Barter's show schedule. Don't miss the opportunity to see a show at this legendary theater.

Early on, to see a show, patrons could pay with produce to see a show at Barter Theatre. Photo courtesy of Barter Theatre.

The building was later turned over to the town, which used the property for town offices and a fire hall, and then it became Barter. Interestingly, there was a fire alarm on the roof of Barter and whenever it sounded the actors were instructed to freeze their position on stage and to resume when it concluded.

Many of the venue's furnishings were salvaged from the old Empire Theatre of New York City before its destruction, according to the Barter Theatre website. When Robert Porterfield learned that the Empire was slated for destruction, he was given one weekend to remove furnishings and equipment for use at Barter. Porterfield and his crew came away with $75,000 worth of seats, lighting fixtures, carpeting, paintings, and tapestries. The lighting system at the Empire, designed and installed by Thomas Edison, was used at Barter Theatre through the mid-1970s.

Barter is the nation's longest-running professional theater and hosts more than two dozen musicals, plays, and live band performances each year.

Barter Theatre is housed in a former church in downtown Abingdon, Virginia.

HIDDEN TUNNEL

Why is there a hidden underground passage in Abingdon?

A Civil War–era tunnel connects the historic Barter Theatre with the neighboring Martha Washington Inn in Abingdon.

The tunnel and all its lore are featured in most tours of the theater, according to Barter, which allows visitors to see it and go into it for a few feet from the Barter side of the tunnel.

It is not possible to walk today from Barter to the Martha via the tunnel because it collapsed and is blocked on the hotel's end. No worries though. Barter and the Martha are across the street from each other in downtown Abingdon, and there is an easily accessible crosswalk on Main Street. The landscaping features numerous statues, including the *Banjo Man* and the *LOVE* sign.

Local lore says the underground tunnel, which was used by various people over the years to connect the two sites, is home to several ghosts, including at least two angry ones. It's said to be haunted by Confederate soldiers.

Barter, which is housed in a former church and fire hall, hosted its first shows in 1933. During the first decade, actors would use the tunnel to reach the hotel, where they stayed while in Abingdon.

The Martha Washington Inn transformed into a hotel in 1935 and has hosted guests like Eleanor Roosevelt, President Harry Truman, Lady Bird Johnson, and Elizabeth Taylor.

The hidden tunnel is featured on most tours of the Barter. Photos courtesy of the Barter.

UNDERGROUND TUNNEL

WHAT: A tunnel once connected Barter Theatre and the Martha Washington Inn in Abingdon, Virginia.

WHERE: 127 W Main St., Abingdon, VA 24210

COST: Price varies

PRO TIP: Tours at Barter Theatre can be scheduled in advance, and most include a visit to the tunnel entrance.

The Martha, named after the nation's first First Lady, was originally built in 1832 as a private residence for General Francis Preston and Sarah Buchanan Preston. The central portion of the present-day hotel consists of the Preston home.

In 1858, the Preston home was sold to become an upscale college for young women, known as the Martha Washington College and known by locals as the Martha, a name still affectionately used today. Most of the inn's ghost stories and legends evolved during the Civil War and the Great Depression—while the college was still in operation. During the war, the hotel became a makeshift hospital for the wounded.

The Martha closed in 1932 and stayed unused for a few years. However, since 1935, the property has prospered as a prominent luxury hotel and even features an 18-hole miniature golf course with its own miniature Martha.

WOLF CAVE

Why are there wolves scattered across the town of Abingdon?

Dozens of painted fiberglass wolf statues are scattered through downtown Abingdon.

The wolf sculptures have decorated lawns and downtown businesses since the project was first created in 2008 by the late Gary Kimbrell as a way to promote Abingdon. Kimbrell had served on the town's planning commission and helped develop Main Street Abingdon, which launched the wolf project.

Known as "Who's Afraid of Virginia's Wolves?," the project began as a fundraiser for the new Main Street group. The wolves were purchased at auction by local residents and businesses.

More than 20 wolves are on display across town.

The campaign was launched due to the legend that the town was once named Wolf Hills by Daniel Boone after his dogs were attacked by a pack of wolves.

Since its first launching, additional wolves have been added to the community's collection.

It should be noted that wolves are now extinct in the Appalachian Highlands and most of the southern United States. Wolves can still be found in the northern and western states. The large canines once ruled the region, but they became a menace to early pioneers, who hunted and eliminated them.

WOLF CAVE

WHAT: Painted fiberglass wolves can be found around Abingdon, Virginia.

WHERE: Throughout Abingdon, VA 24210

COST: Free

PRO TIP: While in Abingdon, visit the historic Tavern, the oldest bar in Virginia and eighth-oldest in the country. The Tavern is located at 222 E Main St., Abingdon, VA 24210.

Looking for wolves? Take a stroll down Plumb Alley in downtown Abingdon, Virginia.

The wolves that attacked Boone and his dogs allegedly emerged from a cave located behind the Cave House. The cave is believed to run underneath the house. The home, also known as the Adam Hickman House, was built in 1857 and can be found at 279 West Main Street. Hickman owned a tannery business making saddles and harnesses.

In recent years, the Cave House has served as an art and craft shop. Be sure to take a stroll on Plumb Alley, where you will find a few wolf surprises.

Visitors can find a variety of wolf artwork around Abingdon, including at the famous *LOVE* sign near Barter Theatre and the Martha Washington Inn.

RETIREMENT HOME FOR SIGNS

Where do vintage signs go to retire?

A storage facility along Lee Highway in Washington County, Virginia, has become somewhat of a vintage sign retirement home.

The famous Robert E. Lee Motel was located between Abingdon and Bristol along Lee Highway. Its neon sign with the General Lee profile picture was iconic. The motel was even one of only three original spots in the country where Colonel Harland Sanders of Kentucky Fried Chicken fame operated a restaurant.

By 2009, however, the motel had become a public safety hazard, and as a result, the county's board of supervisors approved its demolition. It was torn down a few days later, but its unforgettable sign was saved.

The sign has been magnificently restored and is now located at the Bolt Storage facility lot at the corner of Lee Highway and Wood Howell Lane. The lot, previously owned by

VINTAGE SIGNS

WHAT: At least three large vintage signs can be found at a storage lot outside Bristol, Virginia.

WHERE: 16038 Lee Hwy., Bristol, VA 24202

COST: Free

PRO TIP: Looking for more nostalgia? Check out the old Moonlite Drive-In sign, which is located about two miles north on Lee Highway. The theater is now vacant but was recently used to host Barter Theatre stage shows.

Counts began decorating the lot on Lee Highway with vintage signs in 2006 when he opened RC's Storage.

Vintage signs from some of the region's most recognized establishments are now on display at a storage facility on Lee Highway between Bristol and Abingdon, Virginia.

Ronald and Tracey Counts, who restored the sign, also includes nostalgic signs from the Rainbow Autel and Summit Drive-In.

The Rainbow Autel was located about 25 miles away in Chilhowie, Virginia, and the Summit Drive-In was in Glade Spring, Virginia. Both landmarks are now gone, but the signs have been restored and are on display at the storage facility.

Ronald Counts, who previously owned the storage facility, collected many unique signs, including several that have since been auctioned off to the public. He started collecting in 1984, according to a 2016 article in the *Bristol Herald Courier*. He began his collection with antique toys, then began collecting signs and gas pumps.

"It's like anything else–you just keep growing," he said during an auction. "I actually think it's probably a disease. And it ain't just me, it's gotten huge."

Dan Hagberg, who now owns the property, said the signs are "awesome." His company plans to keep them on the property for years to come.

FALLEN OFFICER

What happened to FBI Special Agent Hubert Treacy in Abingdon?

A historic sign in downtown Abingdon marks the spot where a Federal Bureau of Investigation agent was shot and killed by two escapees in 1942.

On March 13, 1942, FBI Special Agents Hubert J. Treacy Jr. and Charlie Tignor attempted to arrest two fugitives who immediately opened fire on the agents. Treacy was killed instantly and Tignor was wounded, according to the marker.

The incident occurred at Pat's Café, a restaurant in Abingdon.

FBI, state, and local officers later captured the men after a gun battle. Army deserters Charles J. Lovett, 22, and James Edward Testerman, 22, were tried, convicted, and sentenced to life in federal prison.

Prior to the incident in Abingdon, the *Knoxville News-Sentinel* reported that the pair beat up a Fort Oglethorpe gun room guard and took four .45-caliber revolvers and 100 rounds of ammunition. Next, they kidnapped a taxi driver in Chattanooga and forced him to drive them to Cleveland, where they dropped him off.

The pair made their way through Knoxville and eventually stopped in Abingdon, where they encountered the FBI agents.

TREACY MARKER

WHAT: A historic marker honoring a fallen officer is located in downtown Abingdon, Virginia.

WHERE: Corner of Wall Street and Depot Square, Abingdon, VA 24210

COST: Free

PRO TIP: There are several art galleries and antique malls nearby, including the working studios at Arts Depot, which is housed in an old freight station, and Zephyr Antiques, which is located in a former theater.

Numerous law enforcement officers have died in the line of duty in the Appalachian Highlands over the years, including a former FBI agent in Abingdon, Virginia.

A memorial plaque was erected in 2017 by the FBI and the Society of Former Special Agents of the FBI, with help from the town of Abingdon. The plaque is located at the corner of Wall Street and Depot Square.

A jury found Charles J. Lovett and James Edward Testerman guilty of murder in April 1942 and recommended a life sentence for both individuals.

TIFFANY & CO. TREASURE

What do Tiffany & Co. and the Great War have in common?

An antique window that can only truly be appreciated from inside the Washington County Courthouse in Abingdon, Virginia, was installed to honor soldiers who fought in World War I.

The courthouse was constructed in 1868, replacing an earlier courthouse that burned down during the Civil War. In March 1919, the Washington County Board of Supervisors approved the manufacture and installation of a one-of-a-kind window to honor the service of local soldiers and their role in World War I. The window replaced a second-floor door, according to documents provided by the Washington County Historical Society.

The window, made of Tiffany stained glass, was installed on July 4, 1919, as part of the town's Independence Day celebration. The design of the window makes the intricate features hard to see from outside. To see it in its entirety, you must go inside and walk up to one of the highest floors of the courthouse. The vibrant glass panels are displayed above a staircase landing and near a chandelier on the way to one of the building's courtrooms.

The window is divided into six sections. The central and largest section depicts a group of soldiers rising from a trench and charging

WASHINGTON COUNTY COURTHOUSE

WHAT: The Tiffany & Co. glass window at the historic Washington County Courthouse in Abingdon is a sight to see.

WHERE: 189 E Main St., Abingdon, VA 24210

COST: Free

PRO TIP: This is an active courthouse, so act accordingly.

Renovations in the 21st century did not affect the Tiffany & Co. stained glass window at the historic Washington County Courthouse in Abingdon, Virginia. Photo courtesy of Bristol Herald Courier.

into battle, according to the Virginia Museum of Fine Arts. Flanking this scene on the left is a cannon representing conflict on land; on the right, a battleship represents conflict on the seas. An American flag is abstracted as a rainbow that arches over the entire span of the window. In the lower, left-hand corner is the emblem for the Red Cross; in the right-hand corner is the emblem for the YMCA.

An inscription across the bottom of the window reads, "To the men and women of Washington County who answered the call of duty in the way of right and liberty."

Tiffany & Co. glass windows can be found at churches around the world, as well as a unique one at the historic county courthouse in Abingdon, Virginia.

THE APPALACHIAN BRICK TRAIL

Why is Damascus, Virginia, known as Trail Town USA?

Thousands of hikers annually pass through Damascus, Virginia, on their way from Georgia to Maine along the Appalachian Trail. Many also pass through on the Virginia Creeper Trail, a former mountain railroad turned hiking trail. In all, seven nationally recognized trails cross through Damascus, giving it the name Trail Town USA.

The town itself is, well, kind of weird, and the residents are proud of that fact. There are numerous hostels, restaurants, art shops, and outfitters for all kinds of activities. Each year, the town also hosts Trail Days, which is described as one of the largest hiking festivals in the country and attracts more than 20,000 visitors.

The Appalachian Trail, also known as the AT, is generally just a dirt trail as it crosses the mountains. In Damascus, however, the trail is paved with bricks, each one featuring the name of a hiker or a loved one. Some of the bricks face north while some face south so that hikers walking in either direction can view them.

The Appalachian Trail Conservancy, which maintains the trail, launched the Community Pathway Project, enabling individuals to purchase engraved bricks that would repave the sidewalk in downtown Damascus. The first phase included only 2,180 bricks, a number that symbolizes the total miles of the trail.

Several trails pass through Damascus, Virginia, including the Appalachian Trail, Virginia Creeper Trail, US Bicycle Route 76, and the Iron Mountain Trail.

Personalized bricks along the Appalachian Trail in Damascus, Virginia, were created as part of the Community Pathway Project.

The AT follows Laurel Avenue through the heart of Damascus, where it passes many hiking-related resources, such as stores and hostels. The town's library and the Damascus Trail Center are also on Laurel Avenue.

Town leaders say the Community Pathway Project has created a more personal connection between the town and the Appalachian Trail.

COMMUNITY PATHWAY PROJECT

WHAT: Engraved bricks can be found along the Appalachian Trail in the town of Damascus, Virginia.

WHERE: Downtown Damascus, VA 24236

COST: Free

PRO TIP: Stop by Trails ARTware for some regional artwork, including unique wood carvings. It is located at 100 E Laurel Ave., Damascus, VA 24236.

THE GREAT CHANNELS

Where can I go on a hike and view remnants of the Ice Age?

Tucked away in the 4,836-acre Channels State Forest in Southwest Virginia are the East Coast's only known slot canyons.

The Great Channels, or just Channels, were created during the last ice age, according to geologists. The approximately 20-acre maze of canyons was created when permafrost and ice carved into the 400-million-year-old soft sandstone, leaving behind a mazelike path through the rocks, geologists say. The Great Channels are reminiscent of slot canyons and gorges in the southwestern United States and the outback of Australia. Unlike the desert locations in the Southwest, this landmark is located within the heart of a vast state forest.

THE GREAT CHANNELS

WHAT: Visit the East Coast's only known slot canyons at the Channels State Forest.

WHERE: Saltville, VA 24370

COST: Free

PRO TIP: Do not go alone. It is best to go with a group, especially one led by someone who knows the Channels.

The Great Channels are located near the summit of Middle Knob on Clinch Mountain, one of the area's highest points.

Hikers are required to take trails to reach the Channels. Plan to wear reliable shoes and consider a hiking pole due to the terrain. One of the best ways to reach this natural wonder is by taking the 5.5-mile Channels Trail, which is blazed in red. Hikers also use the Brumley Trail, according to the Tennessee Eastman Hiking & Canoeing Club.

Be careful while hiking through the canyons as they can become overwhelming due to the mazelike formations.

If you're looking for a challenging yet beautiful hike, check out the Great Channels in Southwest Virginia. Photos courtesy of Virginia Department of Conservation and Recreation.

The forest includes the historic Hayters Knob Fire Tower, which is located atop Middle Knob. The lookout was built by the Civilian Conservation Corps in 1939, and it was maintained and operational for about three decades. It was decommissioned in 1970. Writer Jack Kestner wrote about his time on the tower in multiple books and newspaper articles.

I'LL CROSS THAT SWINGING BRIDGE

Are there any swinging bridges I can visit in Virginia?

Swinging bridges can be found across several rivers and creeks in rural Scott County. In the past, they may have been the only means to cross the waterways, especially during flooding, according to a Scott County Tourism write-up.

Also known as rope bridges or pedestrian bridges, they are often called swinging bridges because the bridges, though strong, will sway beneath your feet as you walk across.

Many of the remaining swinging bridges were constructed and are maintained today by the Virginia Department of Transportation. Others were built by residents who used whatever they could find lying around the farm. Oftentimes, mules, horses, or a team of men had to pull the materials across the river or stream to keep the bridge above water.

For those with the desire to cross one of these swinging bridges, Scott County Tourism provides a list of sites to visit. Be prepared to feel the sway beneath your feet, and if someone else is on the bridge, it is also likely to bob up and down. And yes, most of the bridges are a bit high, so those with a fear of heights might also find them challenging, the organization warns.

SWINGING BRIDGES

WHAT: For a bit of nostalgia, visit one of Scott County, Virginia's, historic swinging bridges.

WHERE: Any local river or creek in Scott County, VA

COST: Free

PRO TIP: Many of the swinging bridges in Scott County are open to the public, but some are on private property and cannot be accessed.

This swinging bridge is located along Copper Creek Road outside of Gate City, Virginia.

Scott County Tourism claims the bridge on Angler's Way Road is one of the easiest bridges for public access. From US Highway 23/58N, turn left onto Angler's Way and follow it for about six miles. Pull over alongside the bridge and make your way across.

Another public bridge can be found along the Clinch River Highway. The bridge is located just past the railroad trestle at the corner of Bridge Street and Dewey Avenue in Clinchport, which also happens to be the least-populated incorporated town in Virginia. Only 64 people call this riverside community home, according to the US Census Bureau.

Swinging bridges can be found in Scott County, Virginia, along Copper Creek and the Clinch River, as well as the Holston River in Washington County.

KEEP ON THE SUNNY SIDE

Bristol is considered the Birthplace of Country Music, but where did the legendary Carter Family come from?

The roadside Carter Family Fold venue may be an obscure attraction to some, but to others it's a bucket-list site where a musically innovative family's influence extends even to today's country music.

Alvin Pleasant "A. P." Carter, his wife Sara Carter, and her sister-in-law Maybelle Carter's first recordings were made in 1927 as part of the Bristol Sessions, a project of producer Ralph Peer that launched the country music industry. The Bristol Sessions and the Carter Family are credited with bringing the industry into being with their traditional mountain sound.

After the recordings were released, the Carter Family quickly gained popularity, not only in the region but around the nation and abroad. Featuring traditional folk songs as well as new compositions, their music resonated with audiences and established the Carter Family as one of the most successful, enduring, and influential groups in music history.

Today, guests can visit the Carter Family Fold, which sits on the land of the original Carter homestead. A. P.'s daughter founded the venue in 1974. The building it still calls home was built in 1976 and opened in 1979, according to the organization.

The A. P. and Sara Carter House, the Carter Homeplace, Carter Store, and the Maybelle and Ezra Carter House are all listed on the National Register of Historic Places.

The home of the legendary Carter Family in Hiltons, Virginia, now serves as a country music venue. Top left photo courtesy of Scott County Tourism. Other photos courtesy of Carter Family Fold.

CARTER FAMILY FOLD

WHAT: The acclaimed Carter Family hails from the Hiltons community of Scott County, Virginia.

WHERE: 3449 A. P. Carter Hwy., Hiltons, VA 24258

COST: Prices vary. Visit carterfamilyfold.org for more information.

PRO TIP: Shows are held practically every Saturday night. Be sure to visit the Carter Family Fold for a schedule of events.

The Carter Family Fold, where Johnny Cash held his final live performance, hosts Saturday evening performances between February and November.

Visitors can also tour the cabin and birthplace of A. P. Carter, which was moved to its current location adjacent to the Carter Family Fold and the Carter Family Memorial Museum.

EIGHTH WONDER OF THE WORLD

What is known as the "Eighth Wonder of the World" in Southwest Virginia?

Former US Secretary of State William Jennings Bryan once called the Natural Tunnel the "Eighth Wonder of the World."

The geologic feature is 850 feet long and 10 stories high, according to the Virginia Department of Conservation and Recreation. This "wonder" was naturally carved through a limestone ridge over thousands of years. Other features of the Natural Tunnel include a wide chasm between steep stone walls surrounded by several pinnacles, or "chimneys," the department said.

In 1893, the South Atlantic and Ohio Railroad constructed tracks through the tunnel, connecting the coalfields of Southwest Virginia with Bristol, Tennessee. The section became known as the Natural Tunnel Route when the Virginia and Southwestern Railroad took over the line in 1899. Many passenger trains would stop to allow people to view the unique tunnel.

NATURAL TUNNEL STATE PARK

WHAT: The 850-foot-long Natural Tunnel is located near Duffield, Virginia.

WHERE: 1420 Natural Tunnel Pkwy., Duffield, VA 24244

COST: $5

PRO TIP: Watch for the trains that still travel through the state park.

The chairlift at Natural Tunnel State Park transports visitors 10 stories down to the boardwalk and observation deck at the tunnel.

The Natural Tunnel is featured in the left photograph, and the replica Anderson Blockhouse, which is located within the state park, is on the right. Photos courtesy of Virginia Department of Conservation and Recreation.

Passenger trains eventually ceased to use the rail line in the mid-20th century. Today, coal trains still use the tracks, which are owned by Norfolk Southern.

The state park features a viewing platform on the tunnel floor from which guests can see the tunnel. It can be reached on foot by hiking down from the visitor's center, or by taking a chairlift.

In addition to the natural wonder, the state park features two campgrounds, cabins, picnic areas, an amphitheater, and gift shop.

Natural Tunnel is also home to the Wilderness Road historic area, which includes the replica Anderson Blockhouse. The original Anderson Blockhouse was built by John Anderson in Carter's Valley in 1775. Anderson's property played an important role in the future of the Wilderness Road and provided a stop for pioneers traveling to Kentucky. An estimated 300,000 people traveled the Wilderness Road in hope of a new start.

REMEMBERING RYE COVE

Where and when did the worst tornado in Virginia history touch down?

On May 2, 1929, a tornado destroyed the two-story wooden Rye Cove School building in rural Scott County. It's recognized as the worst tornado disaster in Virginia history.

RYE COVE

WHAT: The worst tornado in Virginia history struck on May 2, 1929, at Rye Cove School.

WHERE: 164 Eagles Nest Ln., Duffield, VA 24244

COST: Free

PRO TIP: The Nature Center at Rye Cove is on school grounds but is open to the public.

Of the nearly 155 students in or near the school building on that rainy Thursday afternoon, 12 were killed, along with one teacher. Dozens of children were maimed from the crush of debris, or from being hurled into surrounding fields. The rest were left with minor injuries and horrific memories, according to an article in the *Richmond Times-Dispatch*.

Two schools are currently located near the old school—Rye Cove High School and Rye Cove Intermediate School.

A wooden cabin that was used by the Red Cross to distribute aid to the injured at Rye Cove on that day is still located on the grounds and serves as an interpretive site for today's students.

At the intermediate school, a memorial topped by the old school's bell bears the names of the tornado's victims, whose ages ranged from 6 to 24.

The tragedy also lives on in music. Scott County native A. P. Carter came to help and viewed the devastation firsthand. He composed a song called "The Cyclone of Rye Cove," which was

A monument dedicated to a deadly tornado in 1929 sits outside of the Rye Cove Intermediate School in Scott County, Virginia.

recorded by the renowned Carter Family and released later that year.

Rye Cove is also part of the Virginia Bird and Wildlife Trail. The old cabin now serves as a nature center and classroom for students and offers maps of the trail system. The trails meander from open fields to shrub patches and into small stands of hardwood forests.

There are numerous opportunities for wildlife viewing at Rye Cove. Eastern box turtles, butterflies, songbirds, woodpeckers, wild turkey, and white-tailed deer can be seen in the vicinity from the trails.

DEVIL'S BATHTUB

Why do Virginians call this swimming hole "The Devil's Bathtub"?

The Devil's Bathtub once served as a little-known swimming hole in the mountains of Southwest Virginia. It was a secret that local residents kept to themselves for a long time. In recent years, however, the secret has spread and more and more people visit the natural wonder every year.

Many visitors miss one part of the secret, though: it is not an easy hike to reach the Devil's Bathtub. A summer downpour makes Devil's Bathtub a nightmare for inexperienced or unprepared hikers. Rescue crews are often called to the spot to help stranded travelers.

However, with proper gear and a willingness to get wet, Devil's Bathtub can make for a perfect getaway.

The approximately two-mile hike takes visitors across multiple creek beds before reaching the Devil's Bathtub, a bathtub-shaped depression in Devil's Creek. A small waterfall streams into the basin like a faucet.

The Devil's Fork Loop Trail, which takes visitors to the Bathtub, is perfect for backcountry enthusiasts. When visiting the attraction, be sure to choose a sunny day when water levels are low. High water makes for dangerous hiking conditions.

After the first creek crossing, you have the option of going right or left, according to the Virginia Tourism Corporation. The US Forest Service, which owns the land at Devil's Bathtub, has posted a sign that indicates the possible options for visitors. One route takes visitors on a seven-mile round trip with no creek crossings. The other trail is shorter but features 13 creek crossings.

The Devil's Bathtub is a great spot to take a hike and cool down during the hot summer months. Photo courtesy of Scott County Tourism.

Be sure to bring a camera along for the hike, because there are many picturesque sites along the trail and at Devil's Bathtub itself.

SWIMMING HOLE

WHAT: The Devil's Bathtub is a natural pool in the mountains of Scott County, Virginia.

WHERE: Devils Fork Loop Trail, Duffield, VA, 24244

COST: Free

PRO TIP: Be sure to check the weather before heading to the Devil's Bathtub.

WONDERFUL RIVER PARK

How did a lost colony become Virginia's first river state park?

Not many blueway trail state parks exist in the United States, but one in Southwest Virginia, where a Frenchman attempted to establish a colony, is burgeoning.

In the summer of 2021, Virginia Governor Ralph Northam and other leaders launched the Clinch River State Park, Virginia's 41st park. The site includes almost 700 acres along 100 miles of the Clinch River as it flows through Russell, Wise, Tazewell, and Scott Counties. The river, which also flows into Tennessee, is widely considered the most biologically diverse river in North America, and one of the richest habitats for freshwater mussels in the world.

As of 2023, the Clinch River State Park was still in the developmental stages, but there are many other opportunities to check out the river, including one public park area.

CLINCH RIVER STATE PARK

WHAT: Virginia's first river-based state park is located along the Clinch River.

WHERE: Sugar Hill Loop, Saint Paul, VA 24283

COST: Free

PRO TIP: Bring a fishing pole. The Sugar Hill Unit welcomes fishermen to the site.

Rare species in the Clinch River include hellbender salamanders, loggerhead musk turtles, and the green-faced clubtail dragonfly, according to the Virginia Department of Conservation and Recreation.

One of Virginia's newest state parks is located along a 100-mile stretch of the Clinch River. Photos courtesy of Virginia Department of Conservation and Recreation.

The Sugar Hill Unit in St. Paul, Virginia, is open for hiking, biking, and fishing, according to the Virginia Department of Conservation and Recreation, which manages the state park system.

The department reports that Sugar Hill consists of eight miles of hiking trails, a picnic shelter, more than two miles of river frontage with significant cultural and historical attributes, and a loop road that encircles the Sugar Hill area.

The property also contains remnants of a lost 18th-century French settlement.

In 1791, two years into the French Revolution, Baron Pierre Francois du Tubeuf purchased thousands of acres of land in Southwest Virginia and planned to establish a French colony there. He called the new colony St. Marie on the Clinch.

It's no wonder Tubeuf chose the bountiful Clinch River to establish a colony. To appreciate his vision, just check out the various access points along the waterway, such as the Artrip Boat Ramp near Cleveland.

WOODBOOGER SANCTUARY

Did Bigfoot move to the Appalachian Highlands?

Looking for the elusive Bigfoot? Be sure to visit the city of Norton, in Southwest Virginia, where Bigfoot, known locally as the Woodbooger, may be residing.

Spend some time at the Flag Rock Overlook, which is located about three miles from downtown Norton, and you will encounter the giant Woodbooger statue. The statue is a perfect spot for a selfie with the wild beast. Afterward, take a short stroll to the rocky overlook where visitors can see all of Norton.

The story of the Woodbooger in Norton traces back to the filming of *Finding Bigfoot*, an Animal Planet television show. The film crew visited the High Knob area of Norton in 2011.

In October 2014, Norton City Council unanimously approved a resolution seeking to designate a Woodbooger Sanctuary in the city. Councilman Mark Caruso said the city's tourism committee wanted to move forward with the sanctuary designation to increase outdoor recreation in the Flag Rock Recreation Area, which adjoins the national forest lands of High Knob.

The resolution states: "If the elusive creature is as scarce and as rare as is believed by those who seek it, and whereas, if the High Knob and adjoining city of Norton recreation areas are possible habitat for the creature, and whereas, if the creature is,

---

Sightings of Bigfoot, Sasquatch, and the Woodbooger have been reported across Virginia, but have been focused in the southwestern part of the state, according to the Bigfoot Field Research Organization.

as it appears to be, an endangered species" the city is hereby declared a sanctuary for the Woodbooger or Sasquatch or Bigfoot.

The resolution adds: "Be it further resolved, that the city of Norton welcomes all those who seek to find and photograph the creature without causing injury to it or damaging the habitat it may reside."

The Woodbooger legend has spawned the Wood Booger Grill, T-shirts at Home Hardware, and the annual Woodbooger Festival, according to the city. The festival is held each year at the Flag Rock Recreation Area, which also includes a campground, hiking and biking trails, and a reservoir for fishing and paddling.

THE WOODBOOGER

WHAT: Looking for the Woodbooger? It's at Flag Rock Recreation Area in Norton, Virginia.

WHERE: Flag Rock Recreation Area, Norton, VA 24273

COST: Free, except for certain activities

PRO TIP: Be sure to also visit the High Knob Lookout Tower, which is farther south off Virginia State Route 619.

The Woodbooger is depicted in a statue, erected in 2015, at the Flag Rock Recreation Area.

SODA CLOCK

Where is one of the world's only publicly displayed Coca-Cola clocks?

Looking for a rare find in downtown Norton, the small city in the coalfields of Southwest Virginia? A rare Coca-Cola clock sign hangs outside of a brick building in the 600 block of Park Avenue.

No one knows exactly when the red-and-white sign was installed, but it was likely to have been in the 1930s or 1940s. Over the years, the sign deteriorated.

In 2019, Coke Consolidated, the nation's largest Coca-Cola bottlers, began the restoration of the sign through the Ghost Sign Restoration initiative. The company said at the time that it had restored more than 30 murals across the country, but never a metal Coca-Cola clock sign.

The Kinsey Neon & Sign Co., a Roanoke, Virginia-based company that completed the restoration, said it believed the clock was manufactured in 1936.

The clock was originally installed on a building that had once been owned by F. B. Kline, an owner of the Norton Coca-Cola Company. The story of the Norton company appears to have begun in 1902 in Bristol, Virginia, when Milton H. Rush negotiated a Coca-Cola franchise in the Bristol area.

COCA-COLA CLOCK

WHAT: The only known Coca-Cola clock sign can be found in Norton, Virginia.

WHERE: 600 block of Park Ave., Norton, VA 24273

COST: Free

PRO TIP: Check out the clock in the evening while taking in a show at the nearby Park Avenue Theater, which features classic movies and stage performances.

The old Coca-Cola clock sign is located in front of the Glass Slipper Boutique in Norton, Virginia.

Kline took over ownership of the business in the mid-1910s and eventually built a new facility on the corner of Sixth and Seventh Streets in Norton.

Coca-Cola has been bottled at three different locations in Norton, including a historic site at Sixth and Seventh Streets.

COAL MUSEUM

Where can I learn about the history of the coalfields of Southwest Virginia?

Drive the backroads of Southwest Virginia and you are likely to encounter what appears at first to be a ghost town or two. The towns, which still have a few hundred residents, were once thriving communities.

Thousands of people lived around the coalfields of Southwest Virginia, where coal companies established several communities for their employees. Stonega, Keokee, Dante, and Trammel are just a few of the old towns. They had churches, theaters, stores, and schools, just like any other towns at the time.

Their history, and the history of the coal industry, can be found at the Harry W. Meador Coal Museum in Big Stone Gap, a railroad town in the coalfields.

The coal museum was put together, bit by bit, from small treasure troves and individual memorabilia from private homes and buildings in the region. For locals, the museum attempts to describe a personal heritage as well as to give a peek into the past. For others, the museum offers a rich educational experience concerning coal and its direct influence on the local lifestyle, according to the website of the town of Big Stone Gap.

The museum is housed in the private library and study of former author John Fox Jr., who wrote *The Trail of the Lonesome Pine*. Fox lived next door in a home that has also been turned into a museum.

The coalfields region of Virginia is home to at least three coal museums, including the Harry W. Meador Coal Museum, the Dante Coal & Railroad Museum, and the Pocahontas Exhibition Coal Mine & Museum.

Guests can learn about the history of the coal industry at a museum in Big Stone Gap, Virginia. Photos courtesy of the Town of Big Stone Gap.

HARRY W. MEADOR COAL MUSEUM

WHAT: Learn about the coal industry and its effect on Southwest Virginia at the Harry W. Meador Coal Museum in Big Stone Gap.

WHERE: 570 Shawnee Ave. E, Big Stone Gap, VA 24219

COST: Free

PRO TIP: Author John Fox Jr., who wrote *The Trail of the Lonesome Pine*, lived next door. His home has been turned into a museum as well.

Named after former coal executive Harry W. Meador, the home includes photographs, mining equipment and tools, office equipment, coal company items, and a small dentist office from the early 1900s.

"From concept to operation, Mr. Meador was the coal museum," the town website explains. "His love of coal mining and its history is evident throughout, as he personally collected, cataloged, and displayed nearly every exhibit."

WOOLLY MAMMOTH

Where is the southernmost location in the US where woolly mammoth fossils have been found?

A giant woolly mammoth roams the streets of Saltville each winter commemorating the massive mammal that lived here thousands of years ago.

The location for woolly mammoth fossils that is the farthest south in the US is Saltville, which is also thought to be the largest Pleistocene fossil site in North America created during what is more commonly known as the Ice Age.

The man-made woolly mammoth, which is kept year-round near the Museum of the Middle Appalachians, is used each year to determine when winter is coming, much like the groundhog of Pennsylvania. The annual event celebrates the community's history.

For over 220 years, Ice Age fossils have been recovered from the lake beds lying under Saltville's marshes, according to information markers in the Museum of the Middle Appalachians. The first written record of these archaeological discoveries was found in a 1782 letter from Arthur Campbell to Thomas Jefferson describing "bones of an uncommon size."

The Saltville Valley represents one of the earliest localities on record from which fossils of the Pleistocene Epoch have been recovered in North America, according to the museum's website.

The woolly mammoth coexisted with early humans who hunted the species for food and used its bones and tusks for making art, tools, and dwellings. Mammoths are closely related to today's elephant.

A woolly mammoth skeleton is on display at the Museum of the Middle Appalachians in Saltville, Virginia. Photo courtesy of Laken Branson.

MUSEUM OF THE MIDDLE APPALACHIANS

WHAT: The Museum of the Middle Appalachians features numerous unique exhibits, including an Ice Age display.

WHERE: 123 Palmer Ave., Saltville, VA 24370

COST: $5 adults, $3 children, $3 senior citizens

PRO TIP: Take a hike on the 8.7-mile Salt Trail between Saltville and Glade Spring.

The museum covers the 30,000-year history of Saltville from the Ice Age to the Space Age. The Ice Age Exhibit features full-size casts of a mastodon skeleton, a mammoth skull, and a giant beaver. Included on display are bones and fossils of the mastodon, woolly mammoth, musk ox, black bear, horse, small mammals, birds, and fish, according to the museum.

Other exhibits include industrial history, the Civil War, and Native Americans.

The inland saline marsh of Saltville contains salt, one of the most essential ingredients in the world. Since the 1780s, salt has been continuously produced in the town.

DEEP CANYON

Where is the largest gorge east of the Mississippi River?

Only a couple bistate parks can be found across the United States, and one, which features the "Grand Canyon of the South," is located on the Virginia and Kentucky border.

The canyon at 4,500-acre Breaks Interstate Park, a joint operation between the two states, is 1,650 feet deep, making it the deepest gorge east of the Mississippi River.

The park offers something for everyone, ranging from elk watching to whitewater rafting along the Russell Fork, a tributary of the Big Sandy River. The river carved itself through the sandstone more than 250 years ago, creating the majestic canyon, which can be viewed from four scenic overlooks throughout the park. The Stateline Lookout, Clinchfield Overlook, Tower Tunnel Overlook, and the Mill Rock Point Overlook provide some of the most beautiful views you will see in the Appalachian Mountains.

BREAKS INTERSTATE PARK

WHAT: Breaks Interstate Park features the deepest canyon in the eastern United States.

WHERE: 627 Commission Cir., Breaks, VA 24607

COST: $3 day-use fee per car, plus other activities

PRO TIP: Take an elk tour at Breaks Interstate Park.

One of the most fascinating aspects of Breaks Interstate Park is its history. Daniel Boone is credited with discovering the Breaks centuries ago when he attempted to blaze trails to Kentucky. Other legends include the stories of Shawnee Indians using the Pow Wow Cave for secret ceremonies, and Englishman John Swift is said to have buried a fortune in silver within the park's boundaries.

There are several spots at Breaks Interstate Park from which to view the canyon, which has been described as the deepest one east of the Mississippi River. Photo courtesy of the Virginia Department of Conservation and Recreation.

Today, the park features a rustic lodge and campground, as well as a swimming pool, splash pad, hiking trails, fishing areas, and horseback riding stables. You will also discover a herd of elk, which had been removed from the area in the 1800s but was reintroduced in the 21st century. Elk first returned to the area in 1997 when 1,500 Rocky Mountain elk were restored in eastern Kentucky. Virginia began its elk restoration program in 2012.

Breaks officials warn guests that the Russell Fork is not a river for a leisurely float. It features some of the most technical and challenging whitewater paddling in the country. Only experienced whitewater paddlers should attempt any section of the Russell Fork within park boundaries.

WILD PONIES

Where can I see wild ponies in the Appalachian Highlands?

Visitors of Grayson Highlands State Park come for the breathtaking mountain views, lush forests, picturesque waterfalls, and wild ponies.

The park, first established in the Appalachian Highlands in 1965, is now home to dozens of friendly ponies. They were introduced in 1974 to prevent reforestation of the highland balds (hills with no vegetation or tree covering), according to the Virginia Department of Conservation and Recreation. Before its establishment, the park had been used by area farmers to allow animals to graze.

The Wilburn Ridge Pony Association manages the herd. During fall roundups of ponies for an auction held in conjunction with the park's annual Fall Festival, association members check the herd for health problems.

The ponies, which are allowed to run wild within the confines of the park, inhabit the balds. They are very accustomed to humans and rarely stop grazing as hikers pass close by.

Many visitors not only see and photograph the ponies, they also try to touch and feed them, a practice that is against park policy. Visitors are advised not to approach, feed, or pet the ponies. The park warns that the animals may bite or kick if they feel threatened and reminds visitors that human food is bad for the ponies.

When first established, the park was called Mount Rogers State Park due to its proximity to Virginia's highest peak. The park features several elevated peaks, mountain views, balds, meadows,

---

Grayson Highlands State Park features full-service and primitive campgrounds, as well as yurts and a bunkhouse available for rent.

People have been visiting Grayson Highlands State Park for decades to view the wild ponies, which were first introduced in 1974. Photo courtesy of the Virginia Department of Conservation and Recreation.

and rhododendron-filled forests. The park also features 13 different trails and provides access to the Appalachian Trail and the Virginia Highlands Horse Trail.

Grayson Highlands is adjacent to the neighboring Mount Rogers National Recreation Area. The park includes campgrounds and a visitor center.

The park is open daily from 8 a.m. to 10 p.m.

GRAYSON HIGHLANDS STATE PARK

WHAT: Grayson Highlands in Southwest Virginia is home to a herd of wild ponies.

WHERE: 829 Grayson Highland Ln., Mouth of Wilson, VA 24363

COST: Free

PRO TIP: Want to stay the night? Check out one of the park's unique yurt accommodations.

GOD'S THUMBPRINT

Where is God's Thumbprint?

Look at a topographic map of Southwest Virginia, zoom in on Tazewell County, and you might notice "God's Thumbprint."

Encompassing nearly 40 square miles, Burke's Garden is a topographically unique elongated basin rimmed entirely by Garden Mountain, a mountain system which protects the area from modern intrusion, according to the Virginia Department of Historic Resources.

> **BURKE'S GARDEN**
>
> **WHAT:** Forty-square-mile Burke's Garden is a topographical wonder in Southwest Virginia.
>
> **WHERE:** Burke's Garden, VA 24651
>
> **COST:** Free
>
> **PRO TIP:** Burke's Garden is a great spot to take a hike on the Appalachian Trail.

This bowl-shaped valley, also known as "Vanderbilt's First Choice," was carved by nature out of the top of Garden Mountain and features beautiful fertile farmland and wildlife. The valley's many pastures allow for spectacular views across the valley to the encircling mountains.

On a topographic map, or from high above in an airplane, Burke's Garden, which is named after James Burke, looks like a giant thumbprint.

It's been called "Vanderbilt's First Choice" because George Washington Vanderbilt had reportedly first considered Burke's Garden for his Biltmore Estate, which was eventually built near Asheville, North Carolina.

The entire valley and the Burke's Garden Central Church and Cemetery are listed on the National Register of Historic Places. Graves date back to the 1700s. Historic farms dot the landscape.

Not much has changed over the past 150 years, which is why the community also has a substantial Amish population. You

An old general store in Burke's Garden, Virginia, features a hard-to-miss and iconic advertisement on one side. Photo courtesy of Julian Meade via Flickr.

might just encounter a family taking a ride through the valley with their horse and buggy.

Entrance to Burke's Garden can be made from a curvy paved route from the north or a mountainous gravel road from the south. Visitors often visit Mattie's Place on Gose Mill Road or the Burke's Garden General Store. Stop by the Burke's Garden Artisan Guild for a display of local art.

Visit on the last Saturday in September, and you can attend the annual Burke's Garden Fall Festival. The festival features art, crafts, a pioneer camp, entertainment, and food.

The Appalachian Trail is also accessible from Burke's Garden.

James Burke, the community's namesake, buried some potato peelings in the area's fertile soil, according to tradition. Sometime later another group camped at the site and discovered the potatoes, resulting in the area becoming Burke's Garden.

Tennessee–Virginia state line

SOURCES

First Lady's Birthplace: https://www.nps.gov/anjo/learn/historyculture/eliza-johnson-devoted-wife-mother.htm.

Divers' Paradise: https://grayquarry.com/.

***Lady* and the *Doughboy*:** https://jcpublicart.com/lady-of-the-fountain/; http://www.stateoffranklin.net/johnsons/bobcox/lady1.pdf; https://en.wikipedia.org/wiki/Spirit_of_the_American_Doughboy; https://doughboysearcher.weebly.com/the-spirit-of-the-american-doughboy.html; https://doughboysearcher.weebly.com/johnson-city-tennessee.html; https://www.atlasobscura.com/articles/wwi-doughboy-statue.

Mountain Dew: https://www.hmdb.org/m.asp?m=177924; "Mountain Dew Tennessee Historic Marker unveiling Friday, July 19." Johnson City News and Neighbor. Johnson City, Tennessee.

"Wagon Wheel": https://wcyb.com/news/local/johnson-city-mural-catches-eye-of-grammy-winning-band-old-crow-medicine-show; https://www.johnsoncitypress.com/living/artist-completes-mural-in-downtown-johnson-city-breezeway/article_5e1ebbe0-2b6f-11eb-a4b2-3b022073b650.html.

Urban Mountain Biking: https://visitjohnsoncitytn.com/place/tannery-knobs-mountain-bike-park/; https://www.johnsoncitytn.org/residents/parks_and_facilities/tannery_knobs.php; https://gearjunkie.com/biking/mountain-biking-tennessee-tannery-knobs-guide.

Miniature Trains: https://www.etsu.edu/railroad/.

Old Bricks: Museum of Ancient Brick brochure: https://generalshale.com/wp-content/uploads/2022/04/GS-Musuem-of-Ancient-Brick-Brochure.pdf; https://northeasttennessee.org/what-you-must-see-inside-the-museum-of-ancient-brick/.

Tesla Coil: https://visithandson.org/tesla/; https://www.roadsideamerica.com/tip/44988.

Gangster's Paradise: http://www.stateoffranklin.net/johnsons/chicago/chicago.htm.

Daniel Boone "Cilled a Bar": https://www.roadsideamerica.com/story/30343; https://www.hmdb.org/m.asp?m=83060.

The Opry: https://www.boonescreekhistoricaltrust.org/; https://jcnewsandneighbor.com/boones-creek-museum-opry-to-host-event-may-8/.

The Pillory of Jonesborough: Irwin, Ned. "The Washington County Courthouse." Washington County Tennessee Archives. 2018; https://www.heraldandtribune.com/news/history-is-hiding-right-in-front-of-us/article_a436abf8-ff15-5f8a-a106-d4579f5db218.html.

Duncan's Roadside Grave: "Grave of First White Man Buried in State." The Knoxville Sentinel. Sept. 7, 1909.

***Junaluska*:** Church, Teresa. "Dedication of statue time to thank, honor." Johnson City Press. No.30, 1986; https://www.johnsoncitypress.com/renowned-sculptor-returns-to-johnson-city-to-repair-32-year-old-piece/article_84c21dde-7662-5e09-b053-7397e9b0e382.html.

Flag Stop on the Tweetsie: https://www.milligan.edu/2014/06/27/milligan-all-aboard-tweetsie-rails-to-trails-project/.

Granny February: https://www.elizabethton.com/2014/10/31/meet-the-ghost-of-granny-febuary/.

The Labyrinths: https://fpcelizabethton.org/building-and-grounds; https://labyrinthlocator.com/.

Giddyap! Betsy's Upping Stones: Beasley, Ellen. "Elizabethton Historic District." National Register of Historic Places. Aug. 23, 1972.

Not Your Ordinary Library: Keeling, Jeff. "Elizabethton library to open new chapter in city services." Johnson City Press. May 25, 1992; Odom, Ila Ree. US Post Office, Elizabethton. National Register of Historic Places nomination form. March 22, 1983.

Life's a Beach in the Mountains: https://www.fs.usda.gov/recarea/cherokee/recarea/?recid=34924; https://www.fs.usda.gov/recarea/cherokee/recarea/?recid=35000; https://www.dcr.virginia.gov/state-parks/hungry-mother.

Ghost Choir: https://www.elizabethton.com/2021/07/09/the-roan-is-a-story-of-beauty-as-well-as-a-mystery-choir/.

Uncle Nick: Behrend, Fred. "Uncle Nick Grindstaff remembered as hermit." Elizabethton Star. March 30, 1958.

Old Church: https://www.sinkingcreek.org/our-story.

Shady Valley's Treasures: http://www.thesnake421.com/; https://www.fs.usda.gov/recarea/cherokee/recarea/?recid=34934; https://www.thetomahawk.com/news/local/article_cbc846a6-a594-11ed-b2db-3390f3f30dae.ht.

Tennessee's State Song: https://www.lyrics.com/lyric/1870779/Steve+Earle/Copperhead+Road.

Butler Museum: https://www.johnsoncountytnchamber.org/area-info/the-butler-museum/.

Fiddlers' Convention: https://www.muraltrail.com/cgi-bin/tennessee/mountain-city-historic-musical-mural-mile/.

Scary Tunnel: https://www.kingsporttn.gov/sensabaugh-tunnel/.

Don't Stop the Press!: https://www.rogersvilleheritage.org/tn-newspaper-and-printing; https://rogersvilletnmainstreet.com/tennessee-newspaper-and-printing-museum/.

***The River*:** https://rogersvilletnchamber.com/laurel-run-park/; https://hawkinscountytn.gov/parks.html; https://www.imdb.com/title/tt0088007/.

Fish Hatchery: https://www.fws.gov/fish-hatchery/erwin; https://visitunicoicounty.com/unicoi-county-heritage-museum/.

A Horse, of Course!: Norungolo, Dede. "Depot renovations harness wall art." *The Erwin Record*. Sept. 27, 2000.

Grisly Elephant Story: https://www.wbir.com/article/news/local/mary-the-elephant-hanging-100-years-later/51-ee92f081-718d-4da6-bb6d-8be8dbe2b8b6; https://www.npr.org/2019/05/15/722236763/the-town-that-hanged-an-elephant-is-now-working-to-save-them.

Ghost Town: https://www.atlasobscura.com/places/lost-cove-settlement; https://appalachian.org/get-connected/explore-protected-lands/lost-cove/.

The Lost State: https://blueridgecountry.com/archive/favorites/franklins-lost-cabin/; https://www.smithsonianmag.com/smart-news/true-story-short-lived-state-franklin-180964541/.

Bridge Burners: https://www.roadsideamerica.com/story/37206.

To Impeach a President: https://www.senate.gov/about/powers-procedures/impeachment/impeachment-johnson.htm; https://home.nps.gov/anjo/learn/historyculture/visitor-tally.htm.

Cannonball House: https://www.tnvacation.com/civil-war/place/4386/cannonball-house/; https://www.hmdb.org/m.asp?m=69805.

Portable Church: https://www.hmdb.org/m.asp?m=210252; https://www.hmdb.org/m.asp?m=210247.

Runway Cemetery: https://kingsportarchives.wordpress.com/tag/tri-cities-regional-airport/.

Backyard Terrors: https://backyardterrors.com/.

Go Underground!: "Small boys and dark places: Cave wonder is mixed blessing." Kingsport Times. June 11, 1965. https://www.worleyscave.co/; https://discoverbristol.org/attractions/worleys-cave/; https://www.usaraft.com/caving-2/.

Icon of Country Music: Turner, Jessica. "In Search of Lesley Riddle. https://birthplaceofcountrymusic.org/search-lesley-riddle/.

Long Island Iced Tea: https://visitkingsport.com/kingsports-long-island-of-the-holston-home-of-the-original-long-island-iced-tea/; https://www.wjhl.com/news/local/long-island-iced-tea-mural-unveiled-in-downtown-kingsport/.

***Big John*:** https://www.findagrave.com/memorial/57444686/john-dan-barker.

Santa Statue: https://heraldcourier.com/lifestyles/entertainment/kingsport-holds-unveiling-of-santa-statue-by-bristol-artist-val-lyle/article_ed3d5552-a7a9-50c1-a169-cad50b33f8aa.html; https://arts.kingsporttn.gov/events/santas-depot/.

Give Eastman a Hand: https://www.eastman.com/en/media-center/news-stories/2021/old-hand.

Food in a Flash: https://www.foodandwine.com/travel/restaurants/pals-sudden-service-top-burger-chains; https://www.palsweb.com/about.

Stone Castle: Witcher, Sam. "Bristol Municipal Stadium. National Register of Historic Places nomination form. March 13, 1987; http://www2.btcs.org/ths/StudentLife/castle/index.htm; https://explorebristol.com/bank-street-mural/stone-castle/.

Hidden Street: https://explorebristol.com/bank-street-mural/.

Bridge Defender: https://archive.knoxnews.com/news/state/james-keelan-bridge-defender-ep-402657250-357414251.html/; https://archive.knoxnews.com/news/local/confederate-lost-hand-while-guarding-bridge-ep-410712822-359693201.html/.

Caterpillar Crawl: https://believeinbristol.org/uploads/files/catcrawlmap_2014_20150216.pdf; https://discoverbristol.org/attractions/caterpillar-crawl/.

Tennessee–Virginia Line: https://discoverbristol.org/trip_ideas/tenniginia-or-virginessee-visit-bristol/.

Cousin Ernie: https://www.bristolhistoricalassociation.com/erniefordhouse.

It's Bristol, Baby!: https://www.bristolmotorspeedway.com/media/.

Mighty Wurlitzer: https://heraldcourier.com/news/pieces-of-the-past-historic-mighty-wurlitzer-graces-theater-s-stage/article_cde53b3a-020e-5910-b25a-2e6ee27aa293.html.

Forty and Eight: https://heraldcourier.com/news/pieces-of-the-past-bristol-tenn-was-final-resting-place-of-one-box-car-from/article_96a8ce51-9f67-556c-a9a4-79af94b5f404.html.

Hank's Last Stop: http://www.theoriginalburgerbar.com/; https://www.roadsideamerica.com/story/39613; https://discoverbristol.org/attractions/burger-bar/.

Solar Hill: https://www.virginia.org/listing/solar-hill-historic-district/291/.

The Offset and TriPoint: https://www.hmdb.org/m.asp?m=211089.

Old Maude: https://www.fs.usda.gov/recarea/gwj/recarea/?recid=73721; https://vacreepertrail.com/forestservice/greencove.htm; https://www.hmdb.org/m.asp?m=65771.

The Resting Tree: https://dendro.cnre.vt.edu/remarkabletree/detail.cfm?AutofieldforPrimaryKey=1819; https://heraldcourier.com/news/the-resting-tree-an-ancient-tree-shades-the-regions-largest-known-slave-cemetery/article_247f9d5a-ece8-5d4a-9f61-9fe33a03072e.html; https://www.facebook.com/BristolVATN/posts/the-resting-tree-is-an-ancient-tree-located-on-a-stretch-of-land-that-once-was-t/3200624716652302/.

All the World's a Church: https://bartertheatre.com/history/; https://sinkingspring.org/about-us/our-history.

Hidden Tunnel: http://www.themartha.com/history.php; https://www.wjhl.com/haunted-tri-cities/haunted-tri-cities-secret-tunnel-under-barter-theatre/; https://heraldcourier.com/news/pieces-of-the-past-hauntings-reported-at-barter-theatre-train-station/article_d6ead2bb-04eb-5460-be72-991110122e28.html.

Wolf Cave: https://heraldcourier.com/cave-house-shop-has-a-long-history/article_58fd92fa-0937-5d9b-8c8d-6179deab723d.html.

Retirement Home for Signs: https://heraldcourier.com/news/iconic-robert-e-lee-motel-demolished/article_c85dbb6d-3da2-5f1e-92af-a0fd48e0a3ce.html; https://heraldcourier.com/news/local/cashing-in-on-their-collection/article_4dd2dd2c-df97-5820-bee2-15842c91b10e.html.

Fallen Officer: https://www.fbi.gov/history/wall-of-honor/hubert-j-treacy-jr; https://www.odmp.org/officer/13427-special-agent-hubert-j-treacy-jr.

Tiffany & Co. Treasure: https://heraldcourier.com/news/pieces-of-the-past-100-year-old-stained-glass-window-honors-local-wwi-soldiers/article_5a1331be-4228-5bfa-b53e-dab7be2e6904.html.

The Appalachian Brick Trail: https://www.facebook.com/communitypathwaydamascus/; https://heraldcourier.com/lifestyles/damascus-sidewalk-project-links-history-and-community/article_396ed8c0-1c58-58ce-9a07-db3127f3e80c.html.

The Great Channels: https://museumofthemiddleappalachians.org/.

I'll Cross That Swinging Bridge: https://www.explorescottcountyva.org/itineraries/swinging-bridges-of-scott-county/#:~:text=Swinging%20bridge%20is%20located%20next,ford%20the%20creek%20twice%20here).

Keep on the Sunny Side: https://carterfamilyfold.org/; https://www.virginia.org/listing/carter-family-fold/5736/.

Eighth Wonder of the World: https://www.dcr.virginia.gov/state-parks/natural-tunnel.

Remembering Rye Cove: https://dwr.virginia.gov/vbwt/sites/rye-cove-intermediate-school-nature-center/; https://richmond.com/weather/ninety-years-after-virginias-deadliest-tornado-outbreak-the-stories-are-as-chilling-as-ever/article_14efc8e6-dac0-521b-80fe-28dd0d219a92.html.

Devil's Bathtub: https://www.virginia.org/listing/devils-bathtub-%26-waterfall/7792/; https://gohikevirginia.com/devils-bathtub-hike/.

Wonderful River Park: https://www.dcr.virginia.gov/state-parks/clinch-river.

Woodbooger Sanctuary: https://www.nortonva.gov/455/Woodbooger-Sanctuary.

Soda Clock: https://www.timesnews.net/news/local-news/restored-coke-sign-adds-life-to-downtown-norton/article_c0096468-e1b7-5210-b37c-388a3e4dd6c2.html.

Coal Museum: https://bigstonegap.com/things-to-do/local-attractions/harry-meador-jr-coal-museum/.

Woolly Mammoth: https://museumofthemiddleappalachians.org/.

Deep Canyon: https://www.breakspark.com/.

Wild Ponies: https://www.dcr.virginia.gov/state-parks/grayson-highlands; https://appvoices.org/2016/12/15/ponies-of-the-grayson-highlands/; https://visitabingdonvirginia.com/landmarks/an-insiders-guide-to-grayson-highlands-state-park-virginias-land-of-high-peaks-grassy-balds-and-wild-ponies.

God's Thumbprint: https://visittazewellcounty.org/burkes-garden-2/.

Worley's Cave

Beach at Hungry Mother State Park

INDEX

The River Gate City